# WORKING IT OUT

Lessons to Help People with Mental
Illness and Other Disabilities Find
Employment and Empowerment

Marjorie F. Olney, Ph.D.

**Kindle Direct Publishing**

ISBN-13: 9798405711263

Cover design by: Art Painter
Library of Congress Control Number: 2018675309
Printed in the United States of America

*I dedicate this book to Sharon. Who else could it possibly be?*

# CONTENTS

# INTRODUCTION, OR LET'S GET THIS PARTY STARTED

Employment for people with mental illness: People don't talk about it much, but it's an issue. According to the National Association on Mental Illness (NAMI; https://www.nami.org), 21 percent of adults in the US have a mental illness and a quarter of these have a serious mental illness. Moreover, only a fraction of individuals with serious mental illness works (Ackerman & McReynolds, 2005). You might think that these statistics say something about the capacity or desire of people with mental illness to work, but you would be wrong. Most people with mental illness would like to work and could be successful with the right strategies and supports (Bazalon Center, 2014; http://bazelon.org). We even have a whole field of study and practice that is dedicated to helping people with mental illness resolve issues related to work and life: psychiatric rehabilitation. Psychiatric rehabilitation addresses the unique employment and community living needs of individuals with serious mental illness; that is, people whose disability interferes with employment, relationships, and life satisfaction. I don't know about you, but I fit in that category.

*Working it Out: Lessons to Help People with Mental Illness and Other Disabilities Find Employment and Empowerment* was written to give both hope and tangible help to people with mental illness who want to work. I directly address the issue of under- and unemployment of people with mental illness by providing an array of strategies designed to maximize success in job, career, and life. In addition to helping people with mental illness, this book will be a useful guide for individuals with other conditions that affect motivation, organization, and cognition such as autism, brain injury, ADHD, and neurological disorders. Actually, the strategies I share can be helpful to just about any job seeker. The book can be used as a supplemental text for university classes as well as for a resource for clinical professionals. Family members and loved ones of people with mental illness will also find the book enlightening.

## Introduction To Your Author

I live and work with bipolar disorder. Sometimes things get really bad, but, over the years, I have figured out how to manage my symptoms and get the job done. Rather than describing how I manage, I will show you. The following is a journal entry that I wrote in 2009. It gives you an idea of how I experience bipolar disorder, but more importantly, it marks the beginning of my convoluted journey toward recovery from serious mental illness.

### Mentally Ill? Don't Expect Get-Well Cards (Journal Entry)

*Of course*, I knew my two-and-half-week jaunt to American Samoa, and then to New Zealand would do a number on my circadian rhythms, which would then wreck the stability of my mood. Flying across time zones always destabilizes me. With rising anxiety, for months now I have anticipated that a nasty episode would result from my trip. I knew what to expect as I know the "number" well and could dance it in my sleep.

I am beginning to feel better, so I am using this blank page as the table on which to perform a postmortem on this most recent brush with craziness. We returned from our trip on a Tuesday night. To get from New Zealand to California, one flies in a northeasterly direction, over the international dateline, thus gaining back a day and five time zones. So, we arrived in Los Angeles an hour earlier than we left New Zealand. That's a time warp as bizarre as the dance in the *Rocky Horror Picture Show*. This trip continued with a short flight down the coast to San Diego, and then a quick taxi ride to our house and two sulking cats. They had been tenderly cared for in our absence, but no matter. They are, after all, cats.

The first few days, it felt like I was moving through oatmeal. My system was slowed down, I had a headache; I needed naps. That is called jetlag. No big deal, right? Toward the end of the first weekend, the jetlag dissipated and was followed by feeling revved up. This was, and is always, accompanied by the evaporation of sleep, engagement in multiple projects, and a complete and utter loss of insight and judgment. Houston, we have a problem.

Looking back on it, I could have *and should have* called my psychiatrist. He would have seen me that day. I would have had a solution in the form of a pill, which would have cooled my fiery neurons. However, my judgment was not good, so I did not make the call.

Things got much worse: Monday, my friend canceled our lunch date, and my expansive, manic mood immediately morphed into a dreaded mixed episode which combines the impulsiveness, insomnia, irritability, and flight of ideas of mania with the guilt and hopelessness of depression. In my case, you can add delusional thinking, paranoia, visual and auditory hallucinations, along with an intense fear of being alone coupled with an intense fear of being with other people. Yes, this last one *is* a challenge.

These last warning signs popped up one-by-one—stealth symptoms! I had not called my doctor and now I was taking a dip in a lake filled with alligators: I was depressed, irritable, unable to sleep, incapable of even sitting in a chair, and feeling guilty and worthless all at once. Sharon, my partner of several decades, got the worst of it. I whined: "Why didn't you tell me? I knew something was going on! Why didn't you see it? I need you to know and to tell me!" Tall order.

In retrospect, I didn't need Sharon to read my mind; I needed to take care of myself. I needed a tool—something that would allow me to measure my feelings and behaviors against my personal norm. I needed a way to recognize and address my various mood states, calling the doctor in a timely way, knowing what to do to help myself. Heck, if I had had a plan in advance, I would have addressed the problem on my return from New Zealand, not a week later when things were so much worse.

This book is all about strategies that I have used or learned about that allow me to work as a college professor while maintaining a circle of family and friends. I know, this shouldn't be so hard but I can tell you that accomplishing these tasks is like Sisyphus pushing the boulder up the mountain each day. In these chapters, I share what I have learned about from rehabilitation counseling, psychiatric rehabilitation, self-help, and my own experience to explore mental health and career issues. I embark on my disability journey by telling personal stories, sometimes funny, sometimes sad. I use what researchers have learned about managing mental illness to make connections between ideas that have traditionally been relegated to separate "silos" of thought and practice. These are the lessons that I have learned over the years about having a great life and satisfying work despite psychiatric symptoms.

Why this book? Why now? First, employment can be a struggle for people with mental illness. At the same time, it is good for us. Work is good for the pocketbook, good for the brain, and, on average, good on an emotional level. I believe that work has the potential for healing, but that success on the job depends on one's ability to be stable, insightful, present, and able to maintain those pesky relationships.

Work is often the first thing to go when a person experiences psychiatric symptoms. In fact, clinicians and psychiatrists will often proclaim that work is "too stressful" and recommend a life collecting Social Security instead. Admittedly, this is an option, but idleness and poverty seldom lead to happiness, unless, perhaps, you are planning to become a monk. Then it's just fine, I suppose. Second, I believe that much of what I have learned is just plain practical and that it can be of value to people with psychiatric disabilities and their family members (as well as counseling students and professionals—this book should be mandatory reading for them). I have not seen a book like this, so why not write it? But why now?

I am on the verge of retirement with time to write and little to lose by "coming out of the closet" as an educator with a mental illness. Like many people with disabilities, I have spent my career concerned that if anyone knew what I struggled with, they would declare me incompetent, disregarding my abilities and achievements. Therefore, I have been careful how and with whom I disclose. Retirement tips the balance in favor of disclosure.

I am, first and foremost, a professor of rehabilitation counseling whose teaching and research fall within the area of psychiatric rehabilitation. I also manage my very own psychiatric disability—that's sort of my second job. And yes, I call it a psychiatric disability rather than a mental illness. A disability is a permanent set of functional issues and deficits that must be managed, lifelong, whereas illnesses come and go. I have learned over time that my symptoms fall in the former category. They always seem to be lurking around. Some readers will resist the idea of their mental illness being a disability in their lives, but others will readily embrace the idea. Psychiatric disability makes sense to me, knowing I have some issues that will consistently need to be managed. Regardless of the terminology you choose for yourself, I hope this book helps those who, like me, struggle with symptoms that can interfere with job performance, career advancement, and work relationships.

It goes without saying: By definition, a disability has had

a significant effect on a person's life. A disability is marked by significant problems in daily activities and functioning in work, relationships, and community life. However, too often people with mental illnesses such as depression, schizophrenia, or bipolar disorder are in the dark about how to understand, adjust to, and cope with the vagaries of their mental health symptoms. Just think about it: With a disability such as diabetes, the doctor explains to the patient how to monitor their condition and what to do if their blood sugar tests too high or too low. They are taught how to care for themselves through diet, exercise, medication, and carefully monitoring extremities for lesions. Psychiatric disabilities are treated differently by both professionals and society; thus, individuals may find relatively little information on how to care for themselves, how to tell when symptoms are getting worse, or the how to find the accommodations and supports they need to be successful. During many decades of seeking and getting treatment, I never once had the experience of a mental health professional telling me how to monitor my moods, and what to do if I saw any warning signs. I want to change that with this book.

## Framework For The Book

I have compiled 12 lessons that I have found helpful for success on the job and in life. I have summed up my findings in a final summary chapter titled "So What? The Takeaways." I am hoping that the reader comes away from my lessons with a compendium of strategies that they can readily apply or adapt, or can recommend to clients and family members. However, what I report is my story, my strategies, and my lessons. Readers are welcome to pick and choose; to tailor for themselves what is most helpful from what I offer, or to seek different solutions.

Many of the strategies and techniques taught in *Working it Out* such as cognitive behavioral therapy and motivational interviewing were developed by researchers and clinicians specifically to tackle the areas that are most difficult for people with psychiatric difficulties. Others, such as the Wellness Recovery Action Plan (WRAP), were created by "peers," people with psychiatric disabilities who provide services to others with disabilities, to cope with their own symptoms. Still, others are methods that I developed for myself, such as weight management, working effectively, getting the right help, moving toward greater insight, and understanding disability.

In this book I tell stories about everything from interacting effectively with one's supervisor and coworkers to creating a long-range career plan. I invite the reader to join me as I describe how I learned to work *with*, rather than *against*, my natural rhythms in mood, reveal research and concepts with practical application to your life, and engage with you in a journey of discovery.

Each chapter is a separate lesson that can be read independently from the other chapters; each one addresses a different aspect of the psychiatric disability experience, providing specific concepts and strategies that are salient to treatment, work, self-knowledge, and relationships. This book is also a scrapbook of my life with bipolar disorder, peppered with my experiences, my journal entries, messages from loved ones, letters, documents, and snippets of all kinds to provide a window into the recovery process. It includes the views of experts, the wisdom of peers, and best practices in the field, even some of my own research. My hope is that this compilation of ideas will provide a needed resource for people with mental illness who want to work or be more successful. And who doesn't want that? Equally, I hope the book is a resource for family members, coworkers, supervisors, clinicians, and students, all of whom will benefit from the myriad perspectives presented.

Here is what you will find in this book. Lessons 1, 2, and 3 introduce self-management—recovery, the Wellness Recovery Action Plan, and the ins and outs of disclosure. These lessons will equip you with beginners' skills for navigating life and work with a psychiatric disability. Lessons 4 and 5 provide practical advice on the management of medications and side effects, including weight gain. The three lessons that follow, 6, 7, and 8, provide career advice about reasonable accommodations, career exploration, and the skills you'll need in the workplace. Lessons 9, 10, and 11 are all about services and supports: therapy, psychiatry, and informal assistance. Lesson 12 stands alone. In this chapter, I explore my own process toward greater insight, introducing a variety of strategies to increase your self-awareness. The final chapter is a summary of all of the strategies covered in *Working it Out*: Know yourself, know you can work, pay attention to support, add tools to your toolbox, and manage your symptoms.

One word about how the book is written. I write about my own life, I write about what I have learned from reading and research, I make suggestions and provide a range of strategies that have been helpful to myself and others. When I've needed pronouns (and I find that I'm often in need of a good pronoun), to be inclusive, I have generally used *"one," "you"* or *"they"* rather than *"he or she."* My hope is that this non-binary expression, although sometimes funny on the ear, doesn't interrupt your flow of thoughts or mine, so please read on!

# LESSON ONE: RECOVERY, OR SCRATCHING MY WAY BACK TO NORMAL

For a few, psychiatric symptoms come—and then go away forever: one bout of depression or one nasty panic attack, never to return. For these lucky people, recovery is not an issue. For me, recovery has been a tough climb up a rough cliff. And I know now that I will always need to manage my disability, but I didn't always know this. This may not be true for you, but for me, recovery has come in bursts of insight and slow hesitant steps. It has resulted in the realization that I'm in this process of recovery for the long-term. In the introduction, I told the story about a psychiatric episode that resulted from traveling across time zones, and the baby steps that I took to get back on track. Although I've learned to manage my symptoms over many decades through medication, research, experience, and a variety of therapies, I still had a lot to learn. I needed to get a real handle on my disability. This chapter begins with my current history, culminating in my most recent crisis, the one that convinced me that I needed to write this damn book.

In 2002, I accepted a tenure-track position and, with my partner, Sharon, packed up and moved across the country. Following our move, I began to experience mixed states. For me, these are a combination of clinical depression—overwhelming feelings of guilt, worthlessness, and hopelessness and mania—

little sleep, irritability, and racing thoughts. I was energized, paranoid, and feeling simply terrible. This period was followed by phases of real mania with its sense of infallibility, irrationality, and prickliness followed by yet more weeks of depression. All in all, I was not doing well. These issues were compounded when, in 2005, I obtained tenure at my university. I went from high energy anxiety to deep depression that almost cost me my career. I could have predicted this, as depression always follows mania in my life and I tend to fall from the mountaintop of successes and good feelings.

This depression was both different and more devastating than previous ones. I couldn't get over it, I couldn't get under it, I couldn't get around it. With this depression, I developed significant cognitive problems, symptoms that are known in cases of severe clinical depression, yet seldom talked about. Each time I "complained" to my psychiatrist about problems with thinking, memory, and associations, he increased my medications. Each time my medications were increased, I became more incapacitated. My psychiatrist, formerly compassionate and collaborative, became progressively more mechanistic and unfeeling as my symptoms, along with my office visits, multiplied. He may have been angry and frustrated by my apparent refusal to respond to his treatments--a situation that I could hardly control.

Needless to say, my work was suffering as I had gotten to the point where I could no longer conduct a lecture. My PowerPoints, usually a great source of prompts, were meaningless when I viewed them. So, I restructured my classes with an emphasis on group work and discussion. However, I found that even leading a discussion was difficult. I could not remember for more than a couple of seconds what John had said or how it related to Mary's perspective. I could feel memories evaporating as they formed. I was terrified. Amazingly, that year I got the best student evaluations of my career. Go figure. What does that tell you about what students respond to? They appreciate the opportunity to talk more and listening less.

Again, and again, I talked to my psychiatrist about my inability to concentrate and loss of memory. He explained that cognitive losses were common in bipolar disorder, and recommended some supplements such as Gingko Biloba. Did he have literature or at least some references so that I could learn more about what to expect in the future? He had none. When he suggested that the cognitive symptoms I reported might be permanent, I broke down crying in terror and grief. His response to my distress was to silently walk over to his desk and write yet one more prescription.

Now, I was finding it increasingly difficult to get out of bed. Just the thought of it filled me with dread, and on many days, I lay in bed with my eyes open, without moving, for hours at a time. Reading was extremely hard—text seemed like a senseless jumble of words and phrases. I could no longer remember, organize, or link concepts, making both lecturing and research nearly impossible. Considering that I am employed as a professor, this turn of events seemed ironic to me. Moreover, as a rehabilitation counselor educator, I am considered to be the "über expert" on career success for people with disabilities, and it appeared that I was failing to apply even the most basic principles of my craft to my own life situation. I desperately needed help.

My family became increasingly concerned during this period of time and encouraged me to get psychiatric help elsewhere. Sharon, my partner of many decades, was worried that I was overmedicated and my sister, Judith, was ready to stage an intervention. My sister Gini remembered me as follows:

### Gini's Recollection

From my earliest memories, our youngest sister has always been bubbly, verbal, upbeat, engaged. What a shock to experience Marj not entering into our lively and sometimes controversial family conversations, responding to direct questions with a hesitant word or two. She sat on the sofa alone, the Florida sunshine filtering through the blinds, with a vacuous, tentative smile on her face and a vacant look in her sleepy eyes. Who are you – and what have you done with the Marji we know and love? We were concerned – very concerned.

With help, I mustered the mental energy to reach out to a therapist, choosing her by zip code from a list provided by my HMO. Now, I don't recommend this haphazard way of choosing a clinician, but my mental and emotional resources were limited at the time. This amazing psychologist took me under her wing, referring me to a new psychiatrist as well as both a neurologist and neuropsychologist who ruled out organic causes for my cognitive problems. Fortunately, with plenty of help from Sharon, my siblings, my colleagues, my friends, and skilled clinicians, I was able to gather the resources I needed to gradually recover from the crisis.

## The Irony

For over four decades, my field of study and practice has been rehabilitation counseling, a profession targeted to meeting the employment and independent living needs of adults with disabilities. Yet, it took me years to connect my job-related problems with the employment problems experienced by other people with disabilities. We all tend to deny that we're having problems until confronted head-on with the facts—often several times and in a variety of ways—and I'm no different. This book was born when my own mental health crisis made doing my job competently impossible, necessitating some major adjustments. Something just *had* to give.

The bad news: Without help, I was no longer going to be able to function in my career. The good news: I had help-seeking skills, knowledge of the system, and a vast array of effective strategies at my fingertips that would allow me to recover and to re-establish myself as a competent professional in my field.

It was at this crisis point that my seemingly insurmountable difficulties met my extensive knowledge of coping strategies, effective supports, and job accommodations, things I had always thought of in terms of other peoples' needs, not mine. No, these were no longer just a set of skills for others; these ideas and approaches were now critical to my survival as a working adult. Through my reading, work, and research, I had spent a lifetime learning about how others with a disability survived and thrived as employees. Now I got to apply those lessons to myself.

## Through The Recovery Lens

Patricia Deegan, a person with a psychiatric disability and a clinical psychologist, introduced the idea of recovery from serious mental illness decades ago (Deegan, 1988; Deegan, 1996). An intellectual front-runner in the field of psychiatric rehabilitation, Deegan distinguished between recovery (i.e., the active process of understanding and managing one's own disability) and rehabilitation (i.e., the helpful services and supports provided by others) as two sides of the same coin, stating that we need both. She elucidated—for people with disabilities and those who care for and about them— the complexities of recovering from a psychiatric disability. As Deegan (1988) put it:

> It is important to understand that persons with disabilities do not "get rehabilitated" in the sense that cars "get tuned up" or televisions "get repaired." Disabled persons are not passive recipients of services. However, they experience themselves as *recovering* a new sense of self and purpose within and beyond the experience of disability [emphasis in original]. p. 47

According to Deegan, managing a disability, including learning how to take medications, care for one's mental and physical health, manage relationships, and monitor daily activities, is not an all-or-nothing proposition. Indeed, recovery is both a process and an outcome. The day-to-day activities you undertake to monitor and manage moods and symptoms constitute the process of recovery; reaching your goal—a stable, loving relationship, a career, friendships, a coveted achievement —is the outcome. However, no one is ever fully "recovered." The journey toward recovery is what this book is all about.

According to social scientists, recovery is a critical concept which includes:

1. A self-concept that extends beyond illness;
2. Symptom management;
3. A sense of well-being;
4. Optimism;
5. Living a meaningful life; and
6. The opportunity to strive to meet one's potential (Fukui, et al, 2011).

Can you be "in recovery" and still experience symptoms? Certainly. Can you be "in recovery" and still be taking medications? Of course; medication is a key recovery tool and can be extraordinarily helpful to the process. It is rare to hear someone say that they "have recovered" from mental illness, meaning they no longer need the support of others, accommodations, or medications. Recovery embraces all of these things.

As people with disabilities, we have strengths as well as needs for support, and we can engage in recovery, moving toward our life goals. Professionals have often been in the driver's seat, yet, to make recovery a reality, we need to be our own drivers. Move over, helping professional! You can be my navigator but I need to be squarely behind the wheel. Explaining "what makes me tick" should not be usurped by professionals any more than white people have the right to define the experience of people of color or men to define the experience of women. *We cannot hand our lives over to professionals and expect them to make sense out of them.* Our recovery is both our responsibility and our right. We don't have to do this alone, but we do need to be in charge.

There was a moment when I knew for certain that I needed to figure out how to manage my disability on my own. I had seen psychiatrists and therapists, expecting that they would have solutions to the constant mental and emotional upheavals in my life. I finally came to the realization that they could provide guidance, but that I needed to always, as I emphatically wrote before, be in the driver's seat.

**Back to the Story**

I needed to gather what I knew to save myself. Putting my journey of recovery and the lessons I learned along the way into a book was not in the plan, yet I'm glad I kept a journal throughout. Here is one journal entry--written during my period of recovery.

# Recovery (Journal Entry)

On this beautiful late summer dawn, the moon setting, and with a purring yellow cat lying across my arms, I will attempt to write about my experience of recovery. (This little cat is surprisingly heavy.)

As I emerge from my mental health crisis, I am first aware of my newfound capacity to feel—the sun on my skin again, the embarrassment that I had been sick enough for everyone to know. I revel in being freed from the damp gray dungeon. I marvel at my mind as it becomes clever and skilled again. I take pleasure in my daily gains: A phone number remembered here, a connection between concepts there. The unfolding is magical, in the same way watching a new baby is totally absorbing. Yes, you have read the child development books and you *know* what is going to come next. Nonetheless, watching a miracle unfold is captivating.

Lexapro, the drug I like to think of as the gift that keeps on giving...and giving...and giving is one of the most important elements in my recovery. It gave me my life back, and in the process, it also gave me 50 extra pounds. So, as a thoughtful, caring, intelligent person, what do you say to a person who is feebly struggling to get out of her chrysalis, blinking against the splendid, painful sunlight, marveling that she now has wings?

You can say many things. "Welcome back" is always nice. "Tell me about your experience" lets her know that you find her metamorphosis to be a topic worth your time. "How are you doing today" allows her to give you an update on all the new baby antics of her emerging mind. These kinds of conversations can be as much fun for the listener as for the teller.

Alas, my pudgy caterpillar self is painfully aware that she has become a rather zaftig butterfly. So, what is best not to say: "Have you gone to a nutritionist?" "Weight Watchers is supposed to be pretty effective," or "perhaps you just need to exercise more."

Now that I'm released from my metaphorical dungeon, I discover that it had been, in reality, a bomb shelter. Everywhere I look is chaos, a war zone of jumbled relationships and broken dreams. I am regaining my strength, so I will start picking up the pieces and putting things to rights. My partner, steadfast during this crisis just as she's been for twenty-five years of ups and downs, "has my back." It's time to make sense of my work; the languishing projects, the classes, the relationships.

During this period of emergence, my brain continues to do new things. Regaining my memory gives me the most joy. I always could remember faces, people, events, and even numbers. During the crisis, when I encountered people I had previously met, I could not even recognize them. I couldn't remember what had been said to me 30 seconds earlier. Being resourceful, I relied on written information during this time, and on covering my own embarrassment and that of the people who, slightly hurt, said, "I'm Joan. We met at the conference last week." Today, I remember my passwords, my bank account numbers and the dates of upcoming events as well as names and faces. Memory has been a barometer for my recovery.

Even in this world of "multitasking," fundamental changes actually occur slowly, one at a time. Many of us have a one-track mind when it comes to the really big things in life. This is not a limitation of intellectual ability; instead, it is limited mental energy. During recovery, first I attended to work, then family, then my environment. I did not make a conscious choice, most likely just responding to the "squeaky wheels" in my life. Each component of the rebuilding process is exciting— but exhausting. For some reason, processing new insights and new capacities is like moving heavy furniture in my head, and each addition requires that everything else is moved in order for the whole to make sense. It has taken nearly two years to summon the resources to address my medication-related weight gain.

We use the term "in recovery" quite a bit, but recovery is not just a cliché; it is an all-consuming, extremely exacting process, perhaps like mental boot camp, except that there are no rules. Your psychiatrist or therapist can be infinitely helpful, but they cannot tell you how to manage the events and priorities of recovery because they do not know. You cannot say how long it is going to take or who you will be upon your recovery. No one knows.

*One thing we do know: Recovery is a precious gift, like a new baby.*

## So, What Is The Lesson Here?

Despite needing medications, psychotherapy, and various strategies and job accommodations to stay on track, I am, by any measure, successful at work. As I approach retirement as a tenured professor I still love teaching and conducting research, and appreciate the opportunities to work with colleagues and students on projects that are meaningful and helpful.

*Am I somehow more capable than other people with disabilities?* Certainly not. One key advantage is that I've learned so much from studying the experience of disability—that of others as well as my own—and from really listening to my clients, employees, colleagues, study participants, and students over the years, people who taught me how they manage their challenges.

So, our starting point is recovery. For me, true recovery began after my most recent crisis, the one I explore in this lesson. I had already learned how to benefit from therapy and had learned to take medication, an element of my recovery that is perhaps most important. However, until I embraced the idea that managing symptoms and their consequences, my successes and failures were mine to manage with help from others, I was not yet on the road to recovery. For years, I had reached out to therapists and psychiatrists, thinking that they had the secret technique or magic pill that would bring an end to this rollercoaster existence. For certain, I benefited greatly from their help. As I said, medication has been a crucial element for me, as has learning cognitive behavioral techniques (which I introduce later), gaining psychodynamic insights, and having help in the form of case management. With all this assistance, I continued to spin my wheels. I needed to take the proverbial bull by the horns.

For years, I flailed around, looking for something, someone who could put an end to the wretched symptoms— the long stretches of depression, the sleepless manic periods, the terrible mixed states, and most of all, the nearly constant paranoia whispering over my shoulder. I really believed that someone would have the magic pill, the new therapy, and that I would find a doctor with a special skill who would excise this misery. Each time I went to my psychiatrist or my therapist, I honestly believed that they could make it all stop. This turned out to be misplaced hope. All along, I had the tools I needed to get a handle on the chaos.

Bipolar disorder was as much a part of me as brown eyes, greying hair, and my lifelong, unquenchable curiosity. It wasn't going anywhere. I would need to manage my symptoms for the rest of my life. This sense that I alone was in control of my recovery was at once both terrifying and delicious. The shift from outer to inner control was almost tangible—if I could have heard it, it would have fallen into place with a "clunk." I wasn't sure how to deal with this new responsibility. I was the new owner of a disability and now I had to write the manual.

Does recovery mean that we are now totally on our own? That we no longer need those highly trained professionals, powerful methods, and innovative therapies? Not at all. After I reached my epiphany, I was better able to seek and find real help. Through years of trial and error, my psychiatrist (not that first guy) and I finally found a medication, Latuda, with undetectable side effects that was more effective than even Lexapro had been. For many years it has controlled my symptoms better than any drug did previously. I also engaged in a year of cognitive behavioral therapy with a remarkable therapist. I use what she taught me daily and will share it with you.

I still have days when I'm feeling revved up and irritable with mania or weighted down and heart-sick with depression. I now acknowledge those feelings and carefully assess the severity. I use my psychiatric rehabilitation skills to decide what to do. If I'm starting to get manic, I reduce the stimulation in my environment and make sure to get a full night's sleep. If I'm starting to get depressed, I clear my calendar for a day or two, if I can, and just take it easy. Usually, these strategies are sufficient and get me back to feeling more like my old self relatively quickly, but not always. There is nothing simple about managing a psychiatric disability but, and this is important, it is manageable.

For every individual, the strategies will be different; you may need to shower and get to work to help lift a dark cloud of depression whereas I need to putter around at home with no pressures. A good workout at the gym may be effective for you, or lunch with a friend. Taking charge of your recovery means figuring all of this out for yourself.

I can tell you what recovery has been like for me, and I know what it is comprised of, but I can't explain exactly how to achieve it for you. I'm hoping that my story and my lessons provide a treasure map of sorts. The components of recovery are hope and acceptance and responsibility. Hope provides the energy to continue to strive, to persevere and to grow. Acceptance permits us to welcome disability into our daily lives rather than rejecting it, as it tends to fight back when we resist it. Recovery teaches us that although we are not alone, we are ultimately responsible. We are also capable.

What have we learned? Lesson One: recovery is possible and it is both your right and your responsibility. The best therapist in the world cannot do it for you. Medications, the support of family and friends, and even accommodations can only go so far. Powerful strategies and a good bit of insight into yourself will help you recover.

# LESSON TWO: WRAP IT UP, I'LL TAKE IT

During the last ten years, I have learned how to develop and use a Wellness Recovery Action Plan—WRAP—to manage my constantly shifting moods. I have found WRAP to be extremely helpful. It provides a systematic approach to managing my symptoms, evaluating my various states of mind, providing structure and action steps when I need them, and directing those around me when I cannot advocate for myself. Although WRAP was created with psychiatric symptoms in mind, I believe the steps are generalizable to most people and any challenging situation. I am only partially joking when I tell my students that they should have a WRAP to help them manage graduate school.

In this lesson, I share how I monitor and address shifts in mood as well as crises. But first, I'll describe WRAP and discuss why it is critical to be in charge of your own recovery. Whereas, in the last chapter, we focused on recovery as a concept and as a lifestyle, here we center on some of the strategies and skills needed to sustain recovery.

Mary Ellen Copeland was the first to develop a self-help system that fully empowers the person in recovery: WRAP. Copeland, a person in recovery herself, invented this system of care with a group of people with psychiatric disabilities. She did this for herself first, and then disseminated it, mostly through peers. Peer is the current term used for individuals who have the lived experience of psychiatric disability and are trained to provide support, peer counseling, and facilitation. Peers now work in many places that provide services to people with psychiatric disabilities as well as facilitating WRAP and other community groups.

WRAP is a simple written document in which you record how you are when you are feeling well, things you need to do each day to maintain wellness, warning signs and symptoms that indicate a need to take action, what to do in a psychiatric or healthcare emergency, and a myriad of other information that is critical to you and indispensable to your family members, friends, supervisor, and clinicians in the event of a crisis.

WRAP is generally taught in an eight-week class, run by a trained peer. Several individuals with psychiatric disabilities take the class together, discussing their responses to a series of prompts. Upon completion of the class, each participant has identified her/his triggers, developed a daily maintenance plan, identified people in their life who might be a support, and established an advance directive in case of psychiatric emergency. Participants are encouraged to keep their plan with them, revising it as life circumstances change (Copeland, 2018).

WRAP is an applied skills program with the aim of daily use. Designing a WRAP is an opportunity to evaluate what triggers symptoms, how to stay well, which people in your life might be supportive and how you want to be treated, literally and figuratively, if and when you are not able to effectively speak for yourself due to symptoms. WRAP is a flexible document that can be changed as your needs change over time.

Why would you use a self-help plan to learn how to control symptoms and manage crises? In my experience, these issues are not covered much in therapy, and your psychiatrist is generally focused on getting medications calibrated for maximal positive effect and minimal side-effects. Other helping professionals may ask you how you are coping and suggest various helpful approaches, but it all comes down to you. No one will manage your disability but you, so you might as well write a WRAP.

This self-help approach only requires one of two things: A WRAP group—probably the best way to design a WRAP, or the WRAP workbook (www.WRAPandRecoveryBooks.com), a pen and a notebook. Oh, I forgot to mention that there is an app available as well. It's nice to construct your WRAP in a group, but I developed and maintained mine individually. WRAP classes are available in many urban centers, often free of charge, and the benefits of developing your WRAP in a group setting are tremendous: brainstorming together, getting wisdom and ideas from others, benefiting from the knowledge and experience of a trained peer-facilitator, and getting to know interesting people are just a few. I suggest getting the WRAP book whether you are joining a group or developing your WRAP on your own. Regardless of your choices, I encourage you to develop and use a WRAP because it has been effective for me and for other people I know.

WRAP has a goodly amount of evidence to support its efficacy, meaning it has been proven effective through clinical trials (Canacott, et al., 2019; Cook, et al., 2013). However, WRAP is not the only self-management program. Illness Management and Recovery (IMR), Taking Charge, Advance Crisis Management, Florida Self-Directed Care, Empowerment Initiatives, or Recovery, Inc. are alternatives. Like WRAP, IMR has been studied extensively and proven to be effective (Pratt et al., 2014).

## The Components Of Wrap

WRAP is designed to allow individuals to:
1. Improve their ability to take responsibility;
2. Manage and reduce mental health symptoms using self-help techniques; and
3. Learn skills to reach out and use support.
    The components of WRAP are the wellness toolbox, the daily maintenance plan, managing triggers, identifying early warning signs, noticing when things are breaking down, and

crisis planning. I will describe each of these components based on my own self-care plan. These examples will give you an idea of what a WRAP might look like and are not intended to replace a thorough WRAP development process with a peer or using official resources.

## Wellness Toolbox

My wellness toolbox contains all of the strategies I need to do to stay well. It is a comprehensive list of recreational, social, and personal actions that I do to stay well and enjoy myself. Some of these activities, like seeing my psychiatrist for a medication check-up, might happen every few months whereas going to the gym for a good workout and seeing friends would happen several times each week.

## Daily Maintenance

My daily maintenance plan has two components. The first is a list that describes what I'm like when I am well. It may not seem that important, but I know from experience that my feelings and behaviors are distorted when I am manic, depressed, experiencing a mixed state, or feeling very paranoid. It is hard for me to remember what I am like normally when I am in an altered state. This list can also be helpful to friends, family members, and clinicians in the event of a psychiatric crisis. For example, the fact is that I'm a blabbermouth all the time, not just when I'm manic. Knowing that might prevent misdiagnosis. The second component of the daily maintenance plan is a list of all the things I need to do each day to stay well. My list includes daily conversations with Sharon, nutritious meals, time for relaxation, getting dressed in an outfit that I really like, and silly things like watching someone remodel a house on the Home and Garden TV network.

## Triggers

Identifying a list of things that trigger symptoms was more difficult for me than were the other components of WRAP planning. I really needed to study why I seemed to suddenly become manic or depressed. I discovered that these moods didn't just appear out of nothing—they were triggered by something specific. For example, I learned the hard way that traveling across time zones or losing a night or more of sleep will reliably trigger mania whereas having a negative interaction at work can trigger paranoia. My list of triggers is long and it gets longer as I learn more about the things in my inner and outer life that seem to prompt mood swings.

The second part of this section is a list of action steps, things to do if I am triggered. For me, becoming manic requires that I immediately remove myself from any situation in which I might become hostile or make bad judgments. I sometimes need the help of other people to determine if my behavior is manic or justified (sometimes it is both). I've learned from sad experience that if I have to ask, I should really shut up. The other thing I do is make sure to sleep. These actions will usually prevent any real damage.

**Early Warning Signs**

This section of the WRAP is a list of signs that tell me I'm starting to have trouble. I monitor my sleep carefully as working in the night, sleeping less and less each day, and high energy both trigger and indicate mania. Depression is different. An early warning sign that I'm getting depressed is the sensation of a heavy weight in my heart that comes with a rush of negative feelings such as concerns that others are judging me poorly, I have done something wrong, or I am a failure. It makes me laugh that I used to believe these feelings were true. I can now feel them, label them, and address them as symptoms of an illness.

**When Things are Getting Worse**

This is where things get tricky. I can tell when things are getting much worse in terms of depression or mixed states because I begin to have auditory and visual hallucinations. With mania, if I have not addressed it effectively and early, I can no longer tell that my behavior is problematic. I might have stopped sleeping, be engaged in multiple projects, and behave in erratic and hostile ways, but it will be difficult for me to judge.

What do I do in these situations? Hallucinations scare me, so I'm likely to call someone to be with me if I'm alone. Having

Sharon or a friend with me makes me feel safer and allows me to care better for myself by eating well, sleeping, and relaxing. Mania is trickier. I rely on feedback from other people to keep me out of trouble. The people who are close to me know the signs of mania. A real indicator that I'm fully manic is that I will deny it —that's problematic. In those beginning stages of mania, I can tell my behavior is different. After a few days or a week, I can't tell anymore.

**Crisis Planning**

One of the unique aspects of WRAP is "Crisis Planning." In this section, I provide detailed information to my loved ones and clinicians on exactly what I do and don't want to happen if I'm not able to make decisions for myself. It has the name and number of my psychiatrist so that Sharon or a trusted friend at work can contact him if I'm no longer able to advocate for myself. Sharon would be the first person to contact in an emergency, followed by my psychiatrist. So far, Sharon has been able to care for me at home and I have not needed to go to the hospital for care. Thank you, WRAP (and Sharon!).

A WRAP can be developed at any time, but this final section is meant to be carefully written when you are well and shared with key people. It can also be notarized and used as an advance directive. This section is critical for anyone who has been or might be hospitalized as one often loses all control once the wheels are in motion within the medical system. Having a WRAP and an advocate are both indispensable when facing possible hospitalization. For example, the WRAP provides caregivers and doctors and nurses with information on medications that do and do not work for you, hospitals and programs that you prefer, and any doctors or places you wish to avoid.

# What I Learned From My Research

In my own life, WRAP has helped me to stay employed, maintain my relationships, and achieve my goals. I was curious about the benefits of WRAP for others, so I conducted a study of the impact of WRAP on employment for people with psychiatric disabilities. Why employment? I have a lifelong interest in employment and have seen the benefits of work both as a researcher and as an employee. Work does more than deliver a regular paycheck for people: It also provides opportunities for friendships, meaningful activities, and structure. McHugo (2012) noted that "employment promotes recovery for persons with serious mental illness by providing extra income and a valued social role..." He found that people with psychiatric disabilities who work improve faster than those who don't work. I discuss work in greater detail in future chapters, but let me get back to my study.

I interviewed ten people, all of whom had an extensive history with psychiatric disability along with homelessness, substance use, and trauma due to domestic violence and child abuse. These individuals all worked successfully and were in recovery. When asked what factors had helped them to remain successful over time, most talked about how they used their WRAP to help them stay employed. How did they do this?

A key component of WRAP is a list of things you do each day to stay well. One study participant talked about his daily routine of getting up, getting showered and getting to work as one of his daily maintenance tasks written into his WRAP. So, for one individual dealing with bipolar depression, knowing that getting up, showering and getting to work kept him well had the added benefit of assuring his long-range employment. Rather than missing a day or week of work due to symptoms, he had learned that taking those transitional steps toward getting himself to work accomplished two things: He was able to work each day, and he found the routines of his job made him feel better as the day went on. Without the daily routine, this person may not have been able to maintain a job.

Study participants discussed their triggers and their crisis plans, but mostly they talked about two things: The people who loved and supported them, and ways to stay employed.

The relationships were central, and several people said they met their support network through support groups. One woman talked about how she and a couple of friends checked in with each other every day, and that if there was no response to a text, they were "at her door." These women, who met during WRAP training, provided the kind of support that Copeland recommends to all of us.

Work was central to the lives of the people we interviewed, and many of them talked about how they used WRAP to manage stressful situations on the job. One woman put it this way:

> In the work life, if I start getting stressed, it's like, 'Okay, what's stressing me? Is it something I can change? Is it something I can control?' And that's another thing that is talked about in WRAP is that we can't control the world, but we can control ourselves. And…that's a big thing.

So, WRAP can make you ready and able to work, and WRAP can help with the daily stresses of work. When it comes to work and WRAP, there is no downside (Olney & Emery-Flores, 2017).

## That List Of Five People You Can Count On

I have a handful of people who are dear to me. Although Sharon has been my constant companion through my ups and downs in life, there have been others who have walked with me on my journey. My sister Karen, also diagnosed with bipolar disorder, is one of my closest allies. Between New York and California, the phone lines have been buzzing for years. My mother adores me and I adore her. For unconditional love, one can't do any better. My siblings, Tom, Judith and Gini, can be counted on for help, both practical and psychological. I have had other friends over the years who I trust to just come and sit with me when things are really rough. My friend and department chair, Caren, has been a source of support. She even has a copy of my WRAP. It is a surprise to me that friends will step up when needed. Like many people, I tend to isolate myself when I'm doing badly, so I'm always shocked that people will just be with me when I'm not okay.

If you are like me, you hesitate to call on friends for support. My tendency is to nurture my paranoid thoughts about others when I am either in a mixed state or depressed. I talk about how I manage this tendency in the lesson on cognitive behavioral therapy. However, reaching out to others has been a benefit almost 100 percent of the time. Copeland recommends that the WRAP contain at least five people who can be contacted in an emergency. I have not consistently had five people on my list, but I aspire to, and you should too!

Over the years. I have kept a journal on and off. Following is an entry that seemed pertinent to the topic of WRAP and self-management. I thought it would be a good way to round out this discussion.

## Manufacturing Happiness (Journal Entry)

This conversation transpired between my partner and myself at 4:45 AM:

Sharon: "You really need to come back to bed."

Marji: "I know. I just need to write something first. I promise to be back in an hour."

This is after I had not gone to bed until 2:00 AM, and I know from experience that sleeping less than three hours means that I am getting manic. I actually had come to that realization the previous evening when I became obsessed after writing the words "nick" and "knack" in the same sentence (as in "nick knack pattiwack, give the dog a bone").

Now I find it hard to sit in a chair, and I keep popping up as different things pop into my head. It's beginning to sound like popcorn in here. The idea of popcorn popping has now joined nick and knack. On and on it goes.

And, yes, I am taking my medications as prescribed.

Living with an interesting neurological makeup makes for

a life that is distressing but never dull. A clinician once asked me, "What are you like normally?" Yesterday, I told my therapist that I have no idea what I am really like. Oh, I know who I am, without a doubt, but I never know what I am going to be like day-to-day. It would be quite reassuring to know, but that has not been part of my experience.

Recently, I wondered aloud, "Have I ever been 'normal'?" Well, I won't go there. Anyway, as Sharon would say, "Normal is over-rated." I would like, however, to just get used to one state of mind for a while, as long as that state is not depression, as I can't stand so much gravity. I lose all buoyancy. I drown in misery. Hypomania—that state of being just a bit manic—is it all right to just maintain it for all the benefits it brings? Oh, I suppose not. There are no well-used clichés for mania but there should be. Mania is fun and dangerous, depression is dull and painful.

I manage my moods, day-by-day, and week-by-week. It's not just this tendency toward mania that I must monitor, but the precarious dips toward depression. I often wonder how I can better care for myself, how I can control the highs and lows. Therefore, I listen intently to those around me, seeking helpful feedback from the cacophony of voices out there.

Just by serendipity, I was sitting in an airport when I overheard the man next to me say to his companion, "My new goal is to manufacture unhappiness out of nothing." Yes, the quote is wonderfully Woody Allen-esque, but also characteristic of what a person with depression, who sees it but can't stop it, would say to signal his friend that he has a heavy heart, but to do so in a light-hearted manner. After I laughed and wrote this gem down, I considered its importance for a minute. I am a naturally optimistic, happy person with very little fodder for manufacturing unhappiness. Sadness doesn't come naturally. Even when I am depressed I seem more lifeless and dull than sad. As an essentially happy human being, how is it that I can manufacture unhappiness out of nothing? When I visualize unhappiness, it is a sort of antimatter that sucks light and joy out of all it touches.

So, I am on guard against unhappiness. I monitor my moods and reactions. I do whatever I think I need to do to protect myself from the cruel, brutal moods and even the fantastical moods that can suddenly turn ugly. I worry that all this vigilance makes me a bore to be with. I have grown into an emotional hypochondriac. Like the old people I laughed about in my childhood, talking about their surgeries and their bowel problems, I fret and stew about my need "to take care of myself" like an old, infirm lady! It's all-consuming for me, but a drag for everyone around me. Where is the effervescent, carefree—but often hypomanic—girl of my youth? Will there ever be a time when I am neither manufacturing unhappiness nor holding up the production lines?

When we were young women, Sharon and I avoided "the recovery people"—the ones that were in Alcoholics Anonymous —in our tight community. They were hard to go out to dinner with because you couldn't just split the bill ("you had a glass of wine. I'm not paying for it.") They were hard to entertain in our home ("can we offer a beer to Bill if Mary is coming?"). They were always asserting their needs and taking care of themselves, like a bunch of old biddies. I now realize that recovery from serious mental illness is not unlike recovery from addiction. I now walk the same tightrope and fear the same spectacular fall to my ruin. Drama queen! Killjoy! Recovery person!

What does it mean to take care of myself? I have learned from cruel experience that crossing time zones has a deleterious effect on my mood. But here is the dilemma: In October, there are two important conferences on the east coast of the United States. I live three time zones to the west, so I chose the smaller gathering, with people I know and like. Even so, by the end of day two, I was paranoid, hearing voices—*these people are talking about me all over the room*. Now, you know and I know that this is utter foolishness, but it seemed so very real. Was I manufacturing unhappiness out of nothing, making more of that antimatter, zeroing out all my happiness? I know many cognitive behavioral techniques, so I counter and refute these thoughts, but now I feel upset and tired. I can't stand to be with these people any longer. I return to my hotel room, talk to a close friend, go to bed early, sleep well, and wake up feeling fine. Sure, I took care of myself, this time by missing a fun dinner out with colleagues I admire and enjoy. So be it.

When I am very ill with melancholy, I say, "I don't have depression; depression has me," and this is true. When I am beginning to spiral upward, sleeping less, working more, talking a lot, I ask others, "Do I seem okay to you? Am I talking too fast?" "Has the happiness factory gone completely crazy again, like the candy assembly line in *I Love Lucy*?"

My immediate goal is to manufacture *modest* happiness and shut down the misery factory for good. My long-term goal is to manufacture enough happiness to buoy me up and keep me afloat, to give me back some of my youthful joy and carry me far from the old-lady crankiness that is a byproduct of my recovery efforts.

I'm guessing that many readers have not previously had an appreciation for the active work required to manage a psychiatric disorder, and are glad for the insights. A few may think this is a bunch of whining, and can't think of a time when they had such bizarre and self-defeating thoughts. Before my first psychiatric crisis, I was in the latter category. After all, you don't choose psychiatric disability; it chooses you.

WRAP is a way to identify and manage your own symptoms. When I discovered it over a decade ago, I had been looking outside myself to answers to my symptoms. Who could put an end to these endless cycles of ups and downs? Every door that I entered was a dead end. WRAP put the responsibility for symptom management back on my capable shoulders. Ultimately, I needed to take care of the problems. Did that mean that I was all alone in the process? Not at all. Taking responsibility freed me up to use the resources around me more wisely. It allowed me to work more productively with my psychiatrist, trying many different medications before we came up with the perfect combination. It helped me work with my therapist, understanding what she was saying in a new way; not as solutions to my problems but as guidelines for mapping my journey. I was able to hear her with new ears, picking up on methods for managing my moods that I might have missed if I thought of the problem as hers and not mine. Owning a psychiatric disability is daunting and scary, but it also puts you in control and assures that your actions and interventions will work because they are hand tailored by you, for you.

Lesson Two: Take ownership of your recovery by using a WRAP or a similar plan. A plan that helps you identify triggers, symptoms, and strategies will serve you well. Whether it's manufacturing misery in your own depression factory, considering "nick" and "knack" in a clearly manic sentence, or imagining spiders invading your anxiety-ridden dreams, you can take ownership and, paradoxically, get much, much better in the process. That's a WRAP.

# LESSON THREE: DISCLOSURE— TO TELL OR NOT TO TELL? THAT IS THE QUESTION

Having a psychiatric disability means making frequent decisions about what to say to other people, how much to say, when to say it, and how to say it. Like recovery, "coming out" as a person with a disability--any kind of disability--is an iterative process. In my present job, most of my co-workers and many of my students know I have bipolar disorder. The people who work most closely with me have some inkling of what to do if I am having difficulties at work. However, this was not always the case.

When I was first working at my present university, I experienced a lot of severe symptoms of depression with psychotic features, paranoia, and mixed states. I had not told anyone at work about having bipolar disorder or the severe symptoms I was experiencing: I'm sure my behavior was telling them something, but I sure wasn't talking! I had been withdrawn and uncommunicative for several months. One afternoon, we were preparing to meet individually with students when I became overwhelmed; I sat down in a chair and completely shut down in front of all my colleagues. Subjectively,

I was losing touch with reality. I couldn't understand what people around me were saying, and sounds, shapes, and colors were distorted. I was "decompensating," which is the clinical (and often uncomplimentary) term for having a breakdown. Without intending to, I had "outed" myself. After what seemed like forever, I heard a colleague ask me, "Do you need to go home?" I answered yes, gathered my things, and drove myself home. I don't remember this and can't recall driving. Somehow, I got home safely. Note to self: Never drive while hallucinating.

If my colleagues had known I had a psychiatric illness, they would have been equipped to deal with the situation better. If my department chair had a copy of my WRAP (which I had not even written yet). If, if, if...they would have understood the months of withdrawal and strange behavior that came before a breakdown. They certainly would not have allowed me to drive myself home in such a condition.

As illustrated by this story, in the case of a hidden disability such as a psychiatric illness, disclosure can happen with or without your permission. I look back on the day that I lost it in front of all my colleagues with great embarrassment. I wish I had sat down with each person and let them know that I have bipolar disorder and what that means in terms of symptoms and behaviors. I could have told them what to do and who to call in an emergency, and not to let me drive while "decompensating." Even though it would have been embarrassing to disclose, it would have been less humiliating than breaking down, without warning, in front of people who barely knew me. Sometimes, I think my life is a series of ironies. At the time of this episode, I was working on research about how people manage hidden versus visible disabilities. I'll talk more about the research later in the chapter, but first, another story.

## Managing Disclosure

Disclosure is important, but, as I mentioned, it is not a "once and done" proposition. Even with people who know your diagnosis and symptoms, every public revelation of a psychiatric symptom requires some sort of explanation. Here is a journal entry, written after another crisis that happened at work, this time during a meeting. This event occurred a couple years later than the one described previously, and, like it or not, I was clearly "out of the closet" about my disability--many of the people at this meeting had previously witnessed me in a full-blown psychiatric crisis a few years before. However, at the time of this second episode, I still had no plan in place to deal with an emergency. I had not yet discovered WRAP. When the crisis happened, I chose not to disclose. Instead, I snuck away, hoping my friend would cover for me. Here is my account of a crisis with a crappy resolution.

## Anatomy Of An Episode (Journal Entry)

Yesterday morning, I was feeling pretty dreadful but trying to be productive anyway. I try to maintain a normal routine and walk a fine line between listening to my symptoms and what I call the "fake it 'til you make it" strategy. I had slept for five hours but still had that sensation of utter exhaustion: eyes, nose, lips, and throat parched and sandpapery, fatigue settled deep in the core of me like a huge chunk of lead, and a headache. I pushed myself to answer one more email. I was trying to get motivated to get up and get showered for a 10 o'clock meeting. Now that shouldn't be so hard, should it? Sharon had left for work and I was trying to move forward into my day.

I then heard someone walking around my kitchen, "Oh crap! Are the contractors back?" They still have our key and a couple details remain to be done on our kitchen remodel, so this seemed a rational explanation for the sound of heavy footfall coming from my kitchen. Nonetheless, I felt quite alarmed and yelled out: "Hello?" The walking stopped. I jumped up out of bed and hurried down the hall to the kitchen, filled with a mixture of acute anxiety and anger. "Hello? Hello?" No one was there, not even one of our cats that might explain the noise (if the cat were 200-pounds, that is). Then I thought the intruder must be hiding. I checked the back door: Closed and locked. I looked around the house, not a very time-consuming task in a 1,200-square-foot California doll house.

All was as it should be.

I had just experienced an auditory hallucination.

This is never a good sign. For me, "hearing things" and "seeing things" are symptoms of tenuous mental health. These symptoms often come on the tail of paranoia and land right in the lap of major depression. I now felt crazy, crappy *plus* full of dread.

Will I spiral downward?

Most certainly.

What can I do to stop it? Rest? Sleep? Keep going? I don't know.

I call my department chair to get a sense of her feelings about my presence at our meeting. I tell her I'm not feeling well but that I will come if she thinks it is important. She makes a compelling case and I tell her I will be there. The meeting is at a colleague's house, and people are mingling, talking, nibbling bagels, and sipping coffee when I arrive. I join in, making my approximation of normal conversation. We gradually gather around the dining room table and begin our meeting. Throughout this transition, I feel acutely self-conscious, wondering whether my behavior will give away my raw state of mind, my increasingly tenuous grasp on reality.

Candid comments and jokes fly around the room as we work our way through the agenda. I am momentarily caught up in the fun and make a few jokes of my own. I think I said something slightly outrageous and people responded with laughter, but with just a touch of discomfort as well--at least I thought so. I said, in a jovial manner, "No matter how hard I try, I just can't be appropriate. You guys don't know just how hard I try!" There was laughter around the table, and one colleague chimed in, "I know what you mean!" Another maintained a knowing, serious expression on his face and sought eye contact with the guy sitting next to me. And that's what paranoia looks like.

My paranoia continued to build as the minutes turned into hours. I worked very hard at countering the negative thoughts using my cognitive behavioral skills: "It just doesn't matter." "You don't know for sure what ___ is thinking." "You are a loveable and talented person. People like you!" In spite of my best efforts, I became increasingly overwhelmed by a cascade of negative emotions. I started looking around the table to figure out how to get out of there, waiting for a break in the conversation so that I did not jump up and leave right in the middle of a colleague's remarks. Finally, after about two hours of acute misery, I clumsily got up and edged myself along the table. I bent over and whispered in a friend's ear, "Can I talk to you?" He walked with me to the front door and I said, "I am not doing well. I have to leave." He answered, "Don't worry, I'll tell everyone that you were not feeling well. Are you safe to drive?" "Yes, I think so." I really wasn't.

I drove home to the empty house with the strange noises. I contacted our administrative assistant and asked her to cancel my class. I felt anxious and guilty about not fulfilling my obligations to the department, colleagues, and students. I tried to read and found that I couldn't make sense of the jumble on the page. I turned on the television and couldn't even make sense of a decorating show—what's to understand? Finally, I curled up in bed in my clothes and fell into a deep, dull sleep.

I awoke from my nap with the same leaden, sandpapery sensations that I had had that morning. It felt like my emotions were bleeding, they were so raw. I sat in place on the bed, afraid to move. After an interminable period of time, Sharon's car pulled up. I heard her shut her door and lock it with the remote device—"Beep." She came into the house and into the bedroom to find me. "How are you feeling?" I immediately started to feel better.

If you were me in that meeting, would you have disclosed? How would you have said it? Would you have driven yourself home? These are the kinds of questions I used to grapple with constantly. However, there is a very good set of strategies for answering these questions: WRAP. WRAP was introduced in the previous chapter, and, you may recall, one of the components of WRAP is the crisis plan. When my two work crises happened, I did not have a WRAP--I learned about it a couple years later. Timing is everything.

I often wonder how my career might have been better with a crisis plan in place. If a trusted colleague had a copy of my plan and knew what to do, they would have called Sharon right away to pick me up. They would *not* have allowed me to drive home while having difficulty staying in touch with reality. They would have had the numbers for my psychiatrist and my therapist, and known who to call if Sharon couldn't be reached. Perhaps most importantly, if I had a WRAP at that time, I never would have gone to the meeting in the first place. My WRAP clearly states that when I'm having a hard time with depression, I should stay home for a day or two and just rest. I have learned through trial and error that resting can result in the psychiatric symptoms easing significantly. I would have understood that, and I would have been clear with my department chair that I needed a "sick day." Because she would have a copy of my WRAP, she would have known my crisis plan in advance and understood that I was doing the only sensible thing considering my symptoms. If only.

Soon after this second episode at work, I did discover WRAP and I developed a plan. I shared it with my department chair while I was writing it, asking her for her views as an outside observer. I have had a WRAP in place for over ten years now and interestingly, I have never again needed it to manage a crisis. The rest of my WRAP, including the toolbox, daily maintenance plan, and my own advice to myself on how to manage symptoms have kept me well enough to avoid such drama.

**When, Where, and How to Disclose**

A decision to disclose or not to disclose is made each time you meet someone new or experience a symptom that might become "public." This means you are dealing with decisions on whether or not to disclose several times each week. Each meeting with a new person requires a decision: Do I need to say something about my disability? If so, what do I say? What do I omit? If I decide to say something, when should I say it? Is it smarter to leave out some information? How much can I trust people who I tell in confidence? How are others talking about me and my psychiatric disability? Is the talk accurate? Is it enhancing? Disparaging? Stigmatizing? If that's what goes through your head when feeling well, how about when you are experiencing symptoms or feeling very fragile? I have some answers to these questions, but first, let's explore the impact of visibility of disability on disclosure.

# Research On Hidden Versus Visible Disabilities

People with hidden disabilities such as psychiatric disorders need to negotiate disclosure both differently than, and similar to, those who have apparent disabilities. By definition, hidden disabilities are "not immediately noticed by an observer except under unusual circumstances or by disclosure from the disabled person or another outside source" (Matthews, 1994, p. 7). People with hidden disabilities such as psychiatric disorders must deal with the very "hiddenness" of their disability. In my own research, I discovered that, for people with hidden disabilities, disclosure is complicated by the invisibility of the disability (duh!). Interestingly, people with all kinds of disabilities must negotiate disclosure. For example, if a wheelchair user is late for work because their personal assistant didn't show up to help them get ready, they may have to disclose that intimate detail of their life to their supervisor. Regardless of how obvious the disability is to others, deciding what to reveal, when, and to whom takes thought. Both groups feel a need for privacy and find some of their support needs embarrassing (Olney & Brockelman, 2005).

The comparisons and contrasts between living with a visible or hidden disability are further complicated by the perceptions of others. In my research, I found that people with visible disabilities felt that others saw them as less capable than they were, while people with hidden disabilities thought others saw them as minimally disabled or nondisabled. So, on one hand, people with visible disabilities need to demonstrate their competence and, on the other hand, people with hidden disabilities need to demonstrate their need for support. Disclosure is not simple, and there is no one way to manage it.

The disability rights movement, initiated in the late 1960s, brought about social and legislative changes that have dramatically changed the lives of persons with disabilities, both hidden and visible. Individuals with apparent disabilities such as wheelchair users, and people who were blind and deaf, spearheaded this movement, fighting and lobbying to break down the architectural and attitudinal barriers that had kept them out of the mainstream of society, resulting in the Americans with Disabilities Act of 1990 (ADA) as well as the Americans with Disabilities Act Amendments of 2008 (ADAAA), recent legislation that put some of the "teeth" of the original ADA back into law. Individuals with hidden disabilities such as psychiatric diagnoses, learning disabilities, and chronic illnesses were notably absent from this movement. However, we have benefited from the changes that have come about as the result of the disability rights movement. We now have legal recourse in cases of discrimination and are offered reasonable accommodations under the ADA to facilitate our performance in school and work. Technologies that have been developed for individuals with visual impairments have proved beneficial to individuals with learning disabilities, and flexibility in the expectations of employers and educators has improved our opportunities for success both at work and in the classroom.

People with hidden disabilities feel compelled to hide their difference for several reasons. Here are just a few that I have discovered:

1. Disabilities such as psychiatric disorders are viewed by others as being less "authentic" than visible disabilities. People are less likely to "buy" the idea that a person might need extra support or an accommodation if the disability is "all in their head." Disclosure should be approached carefully, knowing that the initial reaction may be to minimize the difficulties one is having. Calibrating the right tone is essential to making sure an individual maintains their dignity and provides a realistic assessment of their support needs.

2. Disclosing one's disability may result in changed perceptions, decreased expectation, or biased behaviors by others. Therefore, disclosure is best done intentionally and carefully, and at optimal times and circumstances, not while losing touch with reality, the way I did it. People might want to plan their meetings at times that they are feeling well so that they can be assertive and calm.

3. Individuals with hidden disabilities sometimes have "internalized oppression," that is, they have accepted negative messages about disability as true, and are unwilling to identify with other individuals who have disabilities. Embracing disability as a valued part of one's identity helps a person disclose their disability in a way that is both understandable to others and enhancing to oneself. It might be better to wait to disclose until one has made sense of one's feelings about disability.

4. A person may view disability as a personal flaw or failure, rather than as a need that deserves to be accommodated

or a difference that should be valued and celebrated. One way to grow as a person is to integrate one's identity as a person with a disability rather than reject and hide it. This stance will invite others to accept and celebrate difference as well. Operating differently in the world can be a source of strength and a benefit to one's organization, family, and circle of friends.

Regardless of the reason, people with hidden disabilities tend to stay silent. The end result is that we are immobilized. Rather than feel affirmed, valued, and connected to a network of social support, we often struggle in isolation. This experience parallels that of persons with physical disabilities five decades ago, before the disability rights movement.

As a researcher, I have seen the possibility of positive change. I have observed that, although people with hidden disabilities do not typically join together, when we do, we validate one another's experiences and reinforce each other's strengths. The "insider talk," shared support, and self-disclosure that emerge from relationships between people with disabilities form seeds of a new understanding of self, and of persons with disabilities as a group. Groups rapidly identify new "norms" and self-definitions, as well as empowering group members toward new understandings, improved adaptations, and an identity distinguished by pride rather than shame. I propose that this "coming together" is the first step in claiming valued identities and roles as persons with authentic needs and strengths. It facilitates "coming out."

It has become apparent to me over the years that succeeding in a career takes much more than simply being assigned tasks one can do, an understanding boss, and job accommodations. In addition to these things, I have had to manage my symptoms and balance my state of mind with my responsibilities, and I have learned never to procrastinate because I can't count on tomorrow. I have discovered the importance of developing a crisis plan and sharing it with key people. I take it easy when I have symptoms, but you may do better going to work--these decisions are as individual as a person's DNA. There is no one answer to the questions concerning disclosure. Learning to feel good about oneself and one's differences provides the healthy backdrop needed for self-acceptance and disclosure. By carefully weighing the pros and cons of disclosure in each situation people can keep themselves safe while providing critical information to the people who need it.

## Coming Out In A Big Way

Wouldn't you know it? I won a big award from the university where I work. This award comes with plenty of fanfare—a short video about my career to be shown at the annual convocation, interviews, media attention, even a photoshoot. And a big decision on my part: Do I come out? Disclosure, as I mentioned, is a never-ending process. You might say, if your colleagues know, your college dean knows, and university human resources knows, who else is there to tell? It turns out that coming out this publicly as a person with a psychiatric illness is a whole new layer of disclosure. It means revealing my disability to *all* of the faculty, staff, and students across campus and beyond.

I decided to go for it. In my two interviews, I talked about having bipolar disorder and how that influenced both my research and my teaching. I talked about how I see mental health services from the "consumer" side rather than the "provider" side, giving me a perspective that alerts students and colleagues to the experience of disability within our society and service systems as second-class citizens. I shared with my interviewers some of the biases I have seen and experienced from counselors and case workers, chief among them an "us versus them" mentality. I discussed my role as a teacher and trainer, and my efforts to sensitize future counselors—to stop themselves from labeling and "othering" their clients—and how my task is complicated by the fact that we must teach the *Diagnostic and Statistical Manual of Mental Disorders, Fifth Edition* (DSM-5) which catalogs every mental illness known to mankind. So, on one hand, I'm telling students to approach new clients with deep respect and as experts on themselves. On the other hand, I'm telling them to find all of the person's problems and reduce the person to a set of symptoms in the DSM-5. No wonder they gravitate to the "us versus them" mentality. I have not yet figured out how to fix this paradoxical situation.

All this to say, I did come out in a big way this time. I was convinced that people will see an accomplished and confident woman who has achieved a great deal in her career, perhaps because of (rather than in spite of) having a disability. During these few months of small-time celebrity, I'm going to do some good with the hand I've been dealt. I am going to tell the world that (a) a psychiatric disability need not limit a person's career success, (b) even the most intractable symptoms can be managed with the right strategies, and (c) employers need not hesitate to hire someone with mental illness, indeed, such an employee may add skills and dimension to the workplace beyond their wildest dreams.

Lesson Three: Disclosure is a complicated, iterative process that should be approached thoughtfully. Having hidden versus apparent disabilities can add to the complexity of "coming out." Proceed with caution, but do proceed.

# LESSON FOUR: MEDICATION, FOR WHAT AILS YA

No one really understands how psychotropic medications work, not even your psychiatrist. We know they interact with our brains. Through some mysterious process, they mediate moods and thoughts and make us feel better. Perhaps there is a committee in our brains that sends out neurotransmitters during their long, convoluted meetings. Maybe they use Roberts Rules of Conduct to make decisions at a neuronal level. Regardless of how they work, I am here to tell you that they can be extraordinarily helpful in the recovery process.

Many people worry that medications might change their personality. In my experience, medications have allowed me to be my authentic self, without the overlay of constant, annoying, and debilitating symptoms. My opinion is confirmed by friends who have had success with psychiatric medications. However, decisions about whether or not to take medications are individual and may take time and experience to form.

As it has been for me, medication may be one of the most important elements in your recovery. Although there are often side effects, and it can be hard to learn how to incorporate medications into one's life, medication will probably be more helpful than unhelpful. In this chapter, I address the skill of taking medications, medication side effects, medication management, and the pros and cons of taking medication.

I am grateful for medications because they enable me to do the things I want to do (and to refrain from doing the things I shouldn't be doing). However, medications do not just impact the targeted neurotransmitters that affect mood and thought, they interact with our brains and bodies as a whole, hence the side effects. Many people feel that medications make them uncomfortable. I say: Go back to your psychiatrist and try a different drug. There is no reason to go around feeling bad when there are so many effective options.

For me, taking medications was a learned skill, one that required years of trial and error to master. Also, taking medications is a complex construct, not simply explained by "adherence" or "non-adherence." People frequently refuse medications, stop taking them, or reduce their dosages for many reasons, including, but not limited to, forgetting, cost, side effects, feeling "altered," weight gain, and concerns about health. Over time, I learned that I functioned much better when I was consistent with taking my medications as prescribed, but it took some bad experiences to get to an epiphany: *hey, the meds really do help.*

## Taking Medications Is A Learned Skill

For me, taking medication was something I learned over time, and I believe this is true for almost everyone. I have tried at least a dozen medications over the years, sometimes taking them consistently, sometimes not. When I analyze my reasons for either taking or not taking medications, the answers surprise even me.

I think many people are concerned that the medication alters them, and I know this was a concern for me, especially before I learned to incorporate medications into my plan. For years, I resisted the idea that my symptoms could be "biological," as my therapist at that time put it. It seemed to me that if I deeply explored the reasons for feeling so terrible, I could stop it on my own. I thought of my mood problems as a growth that could be excised with hard work. It didn't seem real that the mood disorder was integral to me, maybe even in my DNA. When I began taking medications and feeling better, I realized a new truth: the medication allowed me to be *more* myself, not *less*. This realization has happened many times in my life as I experienced different symptoms and tried different strategies to manage them, always coming back to medication as a first-line of defense.

Family members and clinicians are often frustrated when a person goes off their medication. I hear things like, "She was doing so well. Why would she stop taking her meds?" "We might as well admit her to the hospital now." However, the experience of taking medications or not taking medications is more complicated than a simple yes or no response. Sometimes, a person begins to feel better because of medication but fails to attribute the improvement to a pill and instead assumes they are getting better on their own. I have experienced this and can tell you that the thought pattern is not an irrational one. Psychiatric illnesses tend to ebb and flow, and improvements can and do happen without intervention, as do emerging symptoms. To attribute improvement in your emotions, moods, and behaviors to a pill requires something akin to faith. The one-to-one correspondence between medication and improvement may be easy to detect for family, friends, and clinicians, but it is hard to detect for the person taking the pills. Learning the dance takes persistence and practice, on everybody's part, so be patient!

People also express concerns about medications altering their personality, medications perhaps not really helping, and medication side effects. For those of us who have decided to embrace medications, side effects are a big deal. However, I prefer side effects to psychiatric symptoms any day of the week. Nonetheless, I have been known to complain bitterly about perceived side effects —they can be really annoying! I have learned over the years to accommodate medications into my day-to-day life for the value they bring. In the interest of providing you with a balanced report, I do discuss side effects with the understanding that I accept a small amount of inconvenience for a real reward: the ability to function well in my job and life.

## Medication Side Effects

There are lots of different side effects to medications-- rashes, sleepiness, weight gain, sleeplessness, hunger, thirst, the jitters, brain fog--the list could go on and on. Not only that, but much of what I have read about managing medications and their ubiquitous side effects has not been particularly helpful. Using my own experience, I explore ways that I manage certain side effects. In the lesson that follows this one, I address weight-gain, a common side effect of not only medication, but of aging, technology, and living in an affluent society as well. Below is an open letter to clinicians that I wrote in my journal during my recovery. I hope you will forgive the whiny tone and embrace the overall message: getting the meds right is worth your time and effort.

### Dear Mental Health Providers...(Journal Entry)

The next time you say, "Why did you go off your medication? You were doing so well!" consider my "top seven things I hate" list. As a medication-compliant, insightful person with bipolar disorder, I realize the importance of medication to my success, both professionally and socially. Nonetheless, it takes a tremendous amount of sacrifice and determination to stay on medications, and the impulse to just let nature take its course is never far from my mind. The list is roughly in order, starting with the things I hate the very most and ending with the things I simply hate. I would guess that all of your patients and clients have such a list. It might be eye-opening to encourage each one to generate their own and share it with you.

1. The 50 Pound Weight Gain. Over the past several years of being on psychiatric medications, I have gained a net total of 50 pounds. I remember expressing alarm to doctors about gaining five pounds a month and being told, "No, this medication causes *weight loss*, not *weight gain*. You'll just need to exercise more."

2. The Fidgets. Hand tremors, compulsive touching of neck and face, and involuntary moving of lips, hands, feet—a writhing sensation inside. This comes and goes with various medications.

3. Teeth Grinding. More than once, I get to work and realize that I'm out of ibuprofen—needed for the headaches, earaches, and painful jaws caused by clenched my teeth at night. And, then there was the time I got "the fidgets" from the tooth guard my dentist prescribed (see #2).

4. Obsessive-Compulsive Symptoms. The tune "Holly, Jolly Christmas" played in my head for about a year. No, I am not kidding.

5. Trying to Sort it Out. Never being able to tell what sensation is me, a symptom, or a medication side-effect.

6. Difficulty Sleeping. I continue to struggle with sleeping and waking patterns that deviate wildly and whimsically with the slightest change in time zone, hydration, food intake, and exercise. Okay, this may be a symptom.

7. Monitoring by Others. This one is a side effect of medication inasmuch as it is a continual theme. I hate being asked, "Have you taken your medication?"

So, the question is not "How do I get my patient to comply," but "How can *anyone* maintain the fortitude not to *give up*?"

Medication side effects are not simply a nuisance; they become central to every living and breathing moment of our existence. We need to be able to discuss the side effects freely and openly with you each time we visit, as we experience the side effects much more directly than the subtle effects of the drugs on our moods and symptoms. After all, the lived experience that makes "adherence" such an issue for all of us, is that the human mind experiences the subjective *now* as its only reality. It's "now my jaw is tense." "Now I am craving gummy bears" not "hey, my mood is stable and I feel rested."

I value the compassion and expertise of my doctors, and deeply appreciate the effectiveness of my medications. Medication has allowed me to work, to grow, to succeed, and to be a real help to my colleagues, students, family, and friends. In no way would I consider going off my meds; they enable me to function in my job. Work is central to my identity, so being able to function competently makes up for much of the inconvenience.

I do not mean to criticize our helpers, but to shed light on one of their nagging questions: "Why do they go off their meds?" No one really wants to hear about my wardrobe problems and side-effect woes, but these impact the quality of my life in a daily and immediate way. I have seen more denial from doctors—"I've never heard of that side-effect before!" "You must have changed your eating habits." "It's not the meds."—than I have from people who are taking psychiatric medications.

For many, many years now, I've received a service called "medication management." Once every three to six months, I go visit my doctor. My mind is usually in a whirl, trying to figure out what is important to say. If I am not feeling particularly well, I wonder, "What is the most irksome thing in my life right now? Is it a symptom? A side effect? Can I even tell? What can I say in fifteen minutes that will give my doctor enough information to make an educated guess as to the problem and a possible solution?" And, when I am feeling well, I think "Why am I here? I have a helluva lot of work I could be doing instead!"

Over the years, my psychiatrist's most endearing trait has been his enduring belief that he can make me both symptom and side-effect free. In 2014, this dream came true with the introduction of a new antipsychotic drug called Latuda. Before this, I thought my psychiatrist was being funny. So, it is possible to be symptom and side-effect free, but the process required hard work on the part of two people; my psychiatrist and me.

While dealing with intense ups and downs over the past 30 years, I've seen many psychiatrists and therapists, and have been treated for a variety of psychiatric and cognitive difficulties: depression, anxiety, attention deficit hyperactivity disorder (ADHD), and finally, bipolar disorder. I have taken lots of different medications in that time, and they all have had different impacts. Some were easy to live with and some were beastly. What's important is that I have a relationship with my psychiatrist that permits us to do the hard work of finding the right medications that appear to work over months and years.

**The Funny Thing about Psychotropic Drugs**

I wrote the following journal entry just before a medication change. I had been through many different medications but continued to have symptoms and side-effects, a situation that is resolved for now. Medications featured prominently in my journal entries over several years. They were like problematic family members: people I knew and needed, but also couldn't tolerate at times. In this journal entry, I give medications personalities, something that may seem farfetched, unless you have taken psychiatric medications, that is.

# The Names And Habits Of Drugs (Journal Entry)

Abilify. You would think that the word was some obscure, backwoods colloquialism meaning "to make one able," but no, it is the name of a powerful drug that reportedly a) treats manic depression, and b) doesn't cause weight gain. I am going to start Abilify in the morning and will keep you posted on how *able* I feel—to relate to people, to stay on track, to get things accomplished.

I recently joked that drugs are named by the same people who create names for Ikea's products. I imagine a group of creative advertising types pitching their ideas around a fake mahogany conference table: "Heidelfunt" captures the playful, yet functional feel of this lamp, don't you think?" Although the reality of drug naming may be far less exotic, I am guessing that a great deal of thought goes into the name of each new drug, as it represents a fortune spent in research and development and, most importantly, marketing. Hope runs high for the relief of both human suffering *and* red ink.

Like people, all drugs have unique personalities and influences on the lives of those of us who are touched by them. Each psychotropic drug I have taken has meaning for me and each psychiatrist is a magician who is remembered for their particular brand of magic. When I think of a drug that I parted ways with, my mouth will suddenly taste funny, or I'll get a churning sensation in my gut. I don't just take drugs, I get to know them in my body and soul. I live with them day-by-day, gradually learning to understand their benefits as well as their bad habits. Sometimes we become so enmeshed that I can't tell where the drug ends and I begin, but that is another journal entry.

Lithium has been my constant companion for 20 years, with the exception of a year or so during which I went with Depakote. Living with Depakote was very like experiencing the world through a translucent, plastic raincoat that blunted and blurred my emotions and senses. With hand tremors so severe that I couldn't get a fork to my mouth, I never had a chance to see if Depakote would be fattening, as many psychotropic drugs are. Our relationship was fraught with numbness, jitters, and shakes —it never had a prayer. Lithium and I picked up where Depakote and I left off. Because she is an elegant lady, Lithium didn't even ask me where I had been; we just resumed as if nothing had come between us.

As you can tell, I like Lithium. It's true that the drug encourages indulgence and is, therefore, known to cause weight gain. Although easy and pleasant to live with, Lithium can also turn lethal and must be monitored closely. To preserve my health, urbane and sophisticated Lithium is leaving, and her country cousin, Abilify, will be moving in. What will Abilify be like? Will she disrupt my life with her whoops and hollers, or will she be quiet as a country church mouse?

Confronting a drug change raises anxiety. My psychiatrist believes he can both control symptoms and eliminate side effects. I know I smile indulgently each time he says this, as I have lived with drugs and all their shenanigans for a very long time. Changing drugs is not a seamless process. There is the inevitable shouting and door-slamming as one drug moves out and the other moves in. Then, there is the adjustment period as I notice for the first time the habits of Drug X: "Oh, I'm awfully thirsty." "I'm tired—don't want to get up." "Wow, I'm hungry! Barbecue sounds really good." Finally, we settle into a routine together. I note that the new drug is troublesome, but in a different way than the last. When Abilify arrives in the morning, I will lay down the law: "You can abilify me all you want, but don't you dare supersize me. I have a wardrobe of cute outfits in the closet over there and I'd like to wear them again before they go out of style, thank you very much!"

## The Pros And Cons: A Summary

In my view, medication can do two very helpful things. It can reduce symptoms, making it possible to work. It can also make social interactions easier. Those two things, combined, make up most of what we think of as a good quality of life.

Because of symptoms of both mania and depression, I take three kinds of drugs: a mood stabilizer, an antidepressant, and an antipsychotic. In my experience, having medications that control mania is critical to my success. Like WRAP, medications must be tailored to each individual and *my* medications may not be effective for *you*. A good psychiatrist is needed to help find the right combination and dosage for you.

Although I'm very productive when manic, I'm also irritable and grandiose. These characteristics just do not fly in the world of higher education, or any job, for that matter. When manic, I also become irrational and unable to accurately judge what I can humanly accomplish, taking on far too much and starting many projects that go unfinished. Although the false sense of infallibility and boundless energy can be addictive, I have learned through sad experience to forego the lure of mania and settle for a more normal rhythm of life by regularly taking my lithium. Normal for me includes sleeping every night, engaging in work when it makes sense (not around the clock), and interacting with others with human understanding and patience rather than barely-masked fury.

Interestingly, I have gotten much more work done in recovery than I had previously. Mania is, by its very nature, chaotic. Moreover, having mania followed by a mixed state followed by depression seriously gets in the way of productivity and relationships. Therefore, lithium has been my constant companion for decades, and it has served me well. Although I'm not sure exactly how Latuda helps manage my mood, I know it contributes to keeping the mania and depression at bay because I have done so much better with it than without it. My depressions are well-managed with Wellbutrin. Without this medication, I experience periods of crippling depression, making me nearly incapable of doing my job and totally unable to relate to other people.

With all its mischief, life with medication has been richer, happier, and more productive than before. I feel fully myself and seldom sense that I have medications on board. I don't, however, believe for a minute that medications alone can lead to recovery. For that, I need to take an active role in managing my symptoms, engaging with others, asking for what I need, and gaining insight into my thoughts and feelings. The next chapter is the lesson I learned about how to manage my weight gain caused by taking medications (and perhaps aging as well, to be perfectly honest). Weight gain is a common side effect of many psychiatric drugs, so it's good to have a strategy or two to battle the extra pounds.

Lesson Four: Medications can be an excellent recovery tool. It's important to work with a psychiatrist who will continue to try different drugs until you hit a combination that is both effective for reducing symptoms and has minimal side effects.

# LESSON FIVE: THE SKINNY ON MEDICATION-RELATED WEIGHT GAIN

This is a hard topic to write about, both intellectually and emotionally. Quite honestly, it stresses me out. Several times during my adult life, I have dieted, lost weight, even reached my "goal weight," only to promptly and predictably gain it back. I think of extra fat as being the fault of medications, and I'm sure they are a factor. However, gaining weight is a common phenomenon for people both on and off medications. Four years ago, I lost weight and have kept most of it off through vigilance and determination, so it can be done. Here I share my experiences with medication-related weight gain, hoping they will be helpful, or if not helpful, at the very least, entertaining.

One thing that makes the chapter challenging to write is that I am no expert on weight management. I am an expert on employment and disability, and most certainly on my own experience with bipolar disorder, but I'm not a dietician or a medical doctor. I write this chapter based on my understanding and experience alone, and as a learner, not as an expert.

During the course of a year, I lost forty pounds and have kept most of it off. I continue to monitor my weight year to year and every year that goes by without a massive weight gain is a victory. Therefore, this chapter is a detailed account of how I lost weight and what I'm doing to keep the weight off. I don't intend to tell you what you should do or how you should do it, or how to go about the process of weight management. Instead, I write my story in the hope that it will be helpful.

Most professionals suggest that you *simply* "manage your weight through exercise and diet." What a good idea! Why didn't I think of that? As many of us have struggled to lose weight at one time or another, we know what an intractable problem it is. A major side effect of many psychotropic medications is weight gain. Weight gain is probably the factor that most often discourages women (and perhaps men as well) from taking medications as prescribed.

Several times, I have thrown my hands up in despair and ended my efforts to lose weight. The journal entry that follows was written in 2008 after I made a medication switch that resulted in rapid weight gain. The new medication was effective, but even more fattening than the previous one. Of course, silently and swiftly, the weight came on. I had fought the fat, worried about the fat, hated the fat. Here I try to make friends with the fat.

## Love Me, Love My Fat (Journal Entry)

For two years, I have been resisting the weight gain associated with my new medication regime. I spent the first year freaking out about it. The following year, I tried fighting it systematically with an arsenal of strategies. This year I am going to experience it. I'm talking about fat.

Fat is an insulator that seems to have some physical and psychological advantages for the person carrying it around, although you never read or hear about these. I have noticed since my weight gain that fat reduces touch sensation to a remarkable degree. Moving my fingertips from my still lean ribs at the side of my body to my new belly is a revelation. Sensation, strong and immediate over my ribs, becomes muted over the fat areas, almost as if I am touching someone else. The fat does not feel like my own flesh, but like a padded costume I could unzip and step out of.

As I write this, I am reclining, head propped up on a pillow and laptop balanced on belly and hip. I feel a double chin form between my chin and chest, and I find it both disturbing and reassuring. Looking down and seeing a round tummy where there has always been a flat plain of an abdomen also makes me feel slightly gleeful, but I can't fathom why. I am enjoying being fat on some level. At the same time, I have intrusive worries about diabetes, knee problems, fitting comfortably in a coach seat, and having to buy new clothes. I do worry that I look like hell, but as a woman growing up in America, I have had that worry at every weight. I have never had an accurate idea of exactly what I look like.

Weight management requires a great deal of focus and even more time. I think about the women I have known over the years who are tremendously concerned about their weight and appearance. It seems that they seldom excel in other areas of life. From watching my own students, it seems that acute attention to one's appearance competes with attention to academic and professional pursuits. If this desire to look "hot" is evolutionary, and its purpose is to attract and keep a mate, those of us who have achieved those goals—a loving mate and life-long companion, kids or career—should be let off the hook.

In some cultures, once the mate has been procured, people have tacit permission to eat what they want and to attain whatever size they do. The young Tahitians, Samoans, and Hawaiians of both genders are beautiful and sleek. However, there is no truth in advertising there, because many get fat once they "settle down." Culturally, American and European women are expected to remain slim throughout their lifespans, although this is more of an aspiration than a reality, especially on this side of the pond where two-thirds of adults are either overweight or obese. Still, in some American social classes, even women in their middle years and older tend to be "starved to perfection," as my sister Judith quips.

I have had little difficulty ignoring societal expectation in other regards, but the weight gain has proven to be very difficult to accept. I did not marry and have 2.5 kids. Instead, I have lived with a wonderful woman for three decades and have thrown myself into my career. Instead of children, I have students. Instead of beauty treatments, days at the spa, and poring over fashion magazines, I have research to keep me busy in my free time. I live the life of the mind, and I do so without apology. I wonder why, then, I still feel guilty and embarrassed about having become fat. Sharon, my partner, jokes, "because fat is a feminist tissue!"

And why am I both happy about the extra weight and unhappy about it? I have learned a great deal about ambivalence. Drug addicts frequently understand that they need to recover from addiction in order to have the life they desire. However, letting go of the high, their friends, and the security of "business as usual" get in the way of the new, better path. The fact is: I am motivated both to maintain my current weight and to return to my former weight.

I am able to walk around at 205 pounds and not hate myself. I am enjoying the way it feels to be big. Maybe the novelty will wear off and I'll be ready to do the hard work of taking the drug weight off. For now, it is welcome to stay.

Of course, I could not stand to walk around fat for very long. Over the two and a half years that I was fat, I tried many diets, beginning each one with solid commitment and a great deal of enthusiasm. Each one went out with a whimper as weight loss invariably screeched to a halt and discouragement set in. One failed attempt to permanently remove the extra fat was a physician-supervised modified fast. Essentially, all regular food was replaced with "meal replacements," primarily "shakes" that are added in powder form to water and ice and blended. They are pretty tasty, but, as you will read, loaded with the nutrients we call "air" and "water." The dieter is completely restricted to these packaged items, no exceptions, for a minimum of 12 weeks. This is referred to as being "in the box." I wrote this journal entry in July of 2009, while I was actually on this weird diet.

## Welcome To Very-Airy-Liquid Dieting (Journal Entry)

Congratulations! You are about to embark on a quick and easy weight-loss plan: The Very-Airy-Liquid Diet or VALD. The VALD is based on filling foods such as water, air, and ice. These nutritious and delicious foods have been clinically shown to keep you full by expanding to ten times their normal volume upon consumption, thus promoting the satisfying sensation of having eaten a mousse (or is it a moose?). Not only that, with VALD dieting, you can guarantee that all of the water consumed will continue to work its magic through your system at the most convenient moments.

VALD health educators admonish you in your weekly meetings to stay "in the box." Throughout the first 12 weeks, it is imperative that the dieter stay "in the box," which is fully equipped with air, water, ice, a blender, and a lady's room. The box is for the dieter's own protection and should in no way be construed as a prison cell. There are many colors and styles of box available for purchase. Remember, your minimum daily prescription is three quarts of water per day. You will be most pleased with a box that has its own bathroom.

The VALD has been engineered with the busy professional in mind. It is based on the "shake," a dish that is easily concocted in a blender that has been equipped with a jet engine. To create a shake, one begins with water and ice, puts it in the blender, covers it tightly, and turns it on "high." One then adds the "shake" of one's choice, such as chocolate, vanilla, or my favorite, chicken soup (no, I'm not kidding). Note: For the most frothy and delicious shake, blend on high speed for about 10 minutes or until your cat slinks off, meowing pitifully. Your delicious shake is now ready to drink.

The VALD diet is convenient, too. A "shake" can be discretely put together anytime you need a quick pick-me-up *or* risk passing out from hunger. All you need are the key VALD ingredients—air, ice, water and flavoring—and a retrofitted, 40 horse-power blender. These items, of course, fit conveniently into your purse or briefcase. Create a delicious shake during your next meeting. Your colleagues will barely notice the deafening sound as your giant blender does its magic. Or try your hand at creating a shake while driving to the meeting across town—this can be done with ease by attaching your blender to the cigarette lighter adapter available in all makes and models of cars.

As you can see, VALD dieting is pleasant, tasty, and convenient. Pesky decision-making is eliminated, as are variety and excessively-fattening items such as *flavor* and *texture* and *nutrition*. In clinical trials, it was proven that a group of 100 rats preferred the VALD diet to starvation. We are confident that you will love it, too!

I lost over 60 pounds on this draconian diet, but I don't recommend these extreme measures. By the end of the diet, I became quite ill with severe nausea that didn't let up for months. While I was recovering and eating normal food, I gained back nearly every pound. The moral of the story? Be kind to your body and forget the crazy stuff.

## My Solution

On a more serious note, weight management is an enormous issue for many of us who use medications as a key component of our recovery. After years of ups and downs, I had to get real about my health and longevity. I selected a reasonable weight goal that I believe I can maintain for a lifetime. I lost weight. I have maintained my weight for several years. So far, so good! What makes this time different? I'm treating this weight loss as the last one and I'm making changes that should prevent me from gaining the weight back. No more crazy diets, no more throwing my hands up in despair. I work out at a gym three times per week, walk whenever and wherever I can, eat carefully and watch the scale hold steady. I believe weight management, like taking medications, is a learned skill, one that requires trial and error, deep thought, wise counsel, and determination. I know from experience that forgoing medications is not an option for me, so I must continue to control my weight.

Did you notice? I did not tell you to "just lose weight." I know how difficult and complicated that issue is. I understand that weight management is a life-long struggle. I also believe it is worth the effort, so I work at it every day. I have found the Weight Watchers (now called simply WW) plan to be helpful as it can provide necessary structure when I need guidance on what, specifically, helps with weight loss. There is also a strong emphasis on maintenance as well as financial rewards for maintaining your goal weight--you do not have to pay as long as you stay at your designated goal weight. I have also found the support of my sister, Karen, to be indispensable. She and I email constantly about food, dieting, managing social situations (most of which involve food), and exercise--all the topics related to weight management. Being on this journey with another person is extremely helpful, as is having a reasonable goal.

Despite ups and downs in weight and motivation over the years, I am learning how to live with medications while maintaining a healthy weight. That being said, there has been nothing easy about it. For me, both taking psychotropic medications and staying within a healthy weight-range seems to be within reach. However, I find that I must make good choices and be ever vigilant.

I have learned several things about losing weight and

maintaining my goal weight, and I can share them with you. As has been true throughout this book, your experience and needs may be different from mine, but this set of principles has been effective for me for several years now.

1. <u>Set a manageable weight goal, one you can maintain over time</u>. Many people set unreasonable goals and then get discouraged and give up when they can't either meet the goal or maintain it. I went back to the weight I maintained as a high schooler as my goal—not thin, but not overweight either. You might select a weight at which you were most fit or choose another criterion.

2. <u>Follow a plan</u>. Because I am on WW I count points rather than calories, but you can do either. Noom is a great plan that I tried, just to get a sense for it. Find a sensible weight loss plan and stick to it. The pounds will come off—and stay off—if you stick to your plan.

3. <u>Eat mindfully</u>. I not only pay attention to what I'm eating and when. I also pay attention to the flavors and textures of food and I seldom eat something that doesn't taste delicious to me. The calories are just too precious.

4. <u>Lose slowly</u>. When losing, I was happy with one-half to one pound of weight loss each week. As a woman in my sixties, my calorie needs are less. Younger people and men require more calories to stay alive and, therefore, may lose much faster. By adjusting my expectations, a slower rate of weight loss was fine. With perseverance, I eventually reached my weight-loss goal.

5. <u>Stay vigilant</u>. When I was losing, I stuck to my plan. Now that I am in maintenance, I allow myself treats but I still monitor what I eat closely. It's as if your body is a bank account, carefully tracking deposits and withdrawals. It makes no sense to "cheat" because your body will register that candy bar or potato, even if you don't.

6. <u>Monitor intake</u>. When I was losing, I weighed and measured foods to make sure a half-cup of brown rice was exactly that—not two-thirds of a cup, not a quarter

cup, but a half-cup. I don't always do that now, but I have a pretty good idea of how much I'm eating of any given food.

7. <u>Make good choices</u>. Fruits and vegetables never made anyone fat. I use these at every meal to fill me up and help me stay satisfied. I have made friends with salads and I finish each meal, including breakfast, with fruit. When I fill my plate, I make sure that half is covered with vegetables. And, yes, I really do like them all.

8. <u>Eat what works</u>. I eat lots of protein foods because they are satisfying and delicious. I'm not a big fish eater, but I like chicken, shrimp, crab, lean pork chops, eggs, Greek yogurt, and string cheese. I also snack on protein foods when I feel hungry between meals. They make me feel fuller than eating fruit or raw vegetables.

9. <u>Ease up</u>. When I was losing, I limited carbohydrates. Now I allow myself to have a cookie now and then.

10. <u>Work with your natural rhythms</u>. I make sure that I eat on time so that I'm rarely hungry. If you're not hungry, you're less likely to overeat.

11. <u>Be consistent</u>. I eat the same way on the weekends and holidays as I do every other day of the week. As I mentioned, there is no gaming the system.

12. <u>Be assertive</u>. I ask for exactly what I want in a restaurant. Yes, it is a little like the scene from "When Harry Met Sally," but waiters are glad to accommodate. They get lots of special requests and will gladly give you the extra time and attention you need. Some of the things I ask for are "light on the oil and butter," and "please leave the bacon off," and "I'll have that on the side."

13. <u>Monitor your weight</u>. I get on the scale every morning before breakfast. Once every week, I write down my weight so that I have an ongoing record. You may find that having things written down gives you the objective feedback you need when you start thinking that you are not losing weight, or if you need to see the result of

indulging. I can look at my record and see whether I have maintained my weight or it is inching up. This is good.

14. Enjoy moving. I make exercise a priority and I rarely miss. For the past four years, I have gone to the gym three times per week. Could I go four times? I supposed, but three times seems to fit into my life. I spend a half hour on either the elliptical machine or the treadmill to get my "cardio." Then I spend another half hour doing weights. I alternate upper body and lower body exercises each session so that my muscles have time to recover. Exercise can be fun, so try different things until you find a form of activity that delights you, be it line dancing or mountain climbing.

15. Get your steps in. I walk as much as I can. I park far away from the front door to the store, just to get a few more steps in each day, and I walk for fun—on the beach, in the neighborhood, or wherever I am.

16. Make sure you have support. I get support from going to WW meetings and from comparing notes with my sister, Karen. Having Karen diet with me has been an incredible benefit to both of us.

I have adopted a weight loss and weight management lifestyle by both limiting calories and burning calories. I have never maintained my weight for more than a few months in the past, so the coming years will be telling. I believe that I have finally learned how to maintain a healthy weight, but it requires almost the same careful attention that "dieting" does. Perhaps there is no such thing as dieting; dieting means that there is an end to the diet. By adopting the lifestyle changes described in this chapter, I have essentially stopped "dieting" and have, instead, changed my relationships with food and exercise.

Lesson 5: Weight management is a critical task if you notice weight gain related to medications. Because losing and maintaining weight is another learned skill, you may need to try several times in order to get the right combination of strategies that works for you. I believe strongly that you can both maintain a healthy weight and take psychiatric medications. I also know that there is a steep learning curve for both. I invite the reader to try my strategies, and then try different ones if these don't work. What's important, in the long run, is that you're happy and healthy.

# LESSON SIX: ARE YOU ENJOYING THE ACCOMMODATIONS?

Remember the chapter about disclosure? How, as people with disabilities, we are asked to do it over and over again? Never mind that I had previously dissolved into a puddle of tears and hallucinations in front of my colleagues. Ignore the fact that my department chair had a copy of my WRAP and that I had openly shared my experiences with colleagues over the years. It looked like the time had finally come for another dramatic coming out party. Let me explain.

In May of 2012, I was given an incredible gift: promotion to the rank of professor. There will be no more promotions for me. I will never again need to worry about an evaluation of my job performance. Finally, no one can damage my career, just because I have a psychiatric disability. This was the moment for me to share with the university what I had learned during my career as a professional who (also) experiences a psychiatric disability. For the first time in my life, I was uniquely positioned to ask for job accommodations.

With this new stability came new opportunities. However, even with the assurance that my job was safe, I struggled mightily about whether or not to *write it down* and *share it with my employer*, thus making my mental illness official within my place of employment. My colleague, Jae, had been bugging me for years to request accommodations, specifically to help me organize my tasks and keep up with day-to-day requirements. I was always afraid to do so, fearing that the news would get out and my university colleagues would think me less capable because of my need for help. In retrospect, this concern was just plain dumb.

I realize that disclosure in the workplace is more common than dramatic, and I certainly wouldn't mind joining the ranks of visionaries such as Elyn Saks (2007), and Kay Jamison (1996), both of whom are scholars who have made a difference in the world because they disclosed their psychiatric disabilities in their autobiographies. However, in my decision, I considered the unique risks that going public might bring:

1. As a university professor, I interact with circles of people who value the mind above all else. If my mind is less than 100 percent reliable, will they still trust me? Will they think less of my work? Broadcasting my disability may not improve their opinion of me very much.

2. I work with other faculty members who train counselors. In my experience, mental health clinicians are notorious for their "us versus them" mentality, and I worried that my colleagues might see me as a "them." This dichotomous thinking automatically relegates the person with mental illness to a lower social caste, regardless of the competence of that individual. I have observed in recent years that the right-minded movement toward including peer support specialists on treatment teams has sometimes created an underclass of paraprofessionals who are patronized, marginalized, and discredited in the workplace--by clinicians. Announcing my diagnosis may not improve my status at work.

3. Many people think of mental illness as either a bogus malady that makes otherwise perfectly healthy people behave like whining hypochondriacs, or a frightful condition that turns marginal people into public menaces. Every behavior people don't understand is called "crazy." This is probably why so many people confuse mental illness with criminality.

With all these concerns in mind, and with a great deal of fear and trepidation, I moved forward with requesting job accommodations.

## The Interactive Process

Yes indeed, the first thing I did after I got the promotion letter from the university was to initiate the interactive process required by the ADA to procure accommodations. The interactive process is a series of meetings, required by law, during which accommodations are, hopefully, agreed on and granted. Going through our human resources department, I found out who the accommodation officer was and contacted him to learn the procedure for requesting accommodations at my university. I found out that the first step was verifying the disability. I needed a letter from my psychiatrist, explaining my diagnosis. This is exactly why I had not asked for accommodations years earlier--it's so public! Following is the letter from my psychiatrist. In his careful analysis, he leaves little to the imagination.

## Accommodation Letter (Personal Records)

Wednesday, January 09, 2013
To Whom It May Concern:
Re: Marjorie F. Olney

The above patient has been under my psychiatric care for treatment of a severe Bipolar Disorder since November 27th, 2006. I have treated her at monthly intervals and she has been tried on numerous medications, both antidepressants and mood stabilizers. Her disorder has been rather unstable mood-wise, necessitating frequent office visits and medications changes and titrations.

Our goal has been to enable her to function in her personal

and academic life, and to date, we have been fairly successful, despite the frequent occurrence of mood swings. Dr. Olney clearly meets criteria as a qualified worker under the Americans with Disabilities Act.

One of the symptoms of Bipolar I disorder is a sensitivity to time and biorhythm changes. For example, it is not unusual for a person afflicted with Bipolar I disorder to have a major episode, often involving psychosis, following travel through several time zones. A significant alteration in sleep hours and schedule can have a similar effect. Having very stable schedules is extremely important in keeping a person with Bipolar disorder in remission. Dr. Olney has had several major instabilities in her Bipolar disorder triggered by travel and by sleep deprivation/sleep schedule changes. When she stays up much past 9:00 p.m., she is unable to lengthen her sleep cycle, still awakening around 4:00-5:00 a.m., her usual awakening time. Particularly after being "on" for several hours teaching, it is difficult for her to get to sleep much before 1:00 a.m. This sleep deprivation has a significant effect on her mood stability.

I understand that Dr. Olney has been assigned two classes with late hours for the upcoming semester. I also understand for her to perform these duties that she will have to significantly alter her sleep and activity schedule. I have grave concerns that this will result in an exacerbation of her tenuous balance of mood because of her Bipolar disorder, possibility leading to absence from work as we try to re-establish equilibrium with her medications. Because of this, I am requesting accommodations of:

1. No more than one late night class per semester.
2. Reduced workload by one class if there should be periods of sustained depression.
3. Consistent, weekly assistance with managing workload, planning, and organizing.

Thank you for your prompt attention and consideration.
Sincerely,

[Marjorie's Psychiatrist], M.D.
Distinguished Life Fellow, American Psychiatric Association
Clinical Associate Professor of Psychiatry, UCSD School of
Medicine

Once the diagnosis was procured, the interactive process
began with a meeting. I decided to ask my colleague--not just
any colleague, but the gray-haired, highly-respected one--to go
with me, just for a little bit of extra clout. Employers use the
interactive process to (1) determine what accommodation is
needed to fulfill the "essential functions" of the job, (2) decide
whether the requested accommodations are "reasonable," and
(3) begin monitoring the effectiveness of the accommodation if
granted.

## Preparing For The Meeting

The most difficult part of the process was figuring out
what I really needed on the job. Staying organized had been an
ongoing issue regardless of mood state, so I figured an assistant
a few hours per week would be helpful. Another difficulty I
had was teaching late night classes. I couldn't fall asleep on
the nights that I taught until 10:00 which destabilized my
mood. I brought a list of job duties and accommodation needs
to the first meeting. I recall being very nervous and very glad
to have my distinguished colleague with me. I made a point
of specifying the things for which I both needed and didn't
need accommodations, making it clear that I had the skills and
abilities to do the essential functions of the job. It is important to
note that I reviewed every aspect of my job and stated whether
or not I needed an accommodation to manage it. I would suggest
that you thoroughly and reasonably evaluate your tasks and
responsibilities similarly, showing up for the interactive process
meeting fully prepared to negotiate. It won't hurt to bring a
highly respected friend along either.
**The Decision**

Although I anticipated difficulties and felt exposed talking about my disability with university officials, I was granted an assistant as well as the promise of no more than one late-night class per week, which is manageable. I was not granted an accommodation of a decreased workload during periods of exacerbation, although I would have attempted to negotiate this point if I were ever in the situation of needing a reduced workload.

I decided to select a graduate student rather than an undergraduate and hired a mature person who already knew about my disability. I have since had two additional assistants consecutively, all three of whom have been a tremendous help. The accommodations worked out so well that I canceled the third meeting of our interactive process, one that had been scheduled to follow-up and make any needed adjustments. I wrote to the following to the committee:

## Letter To Interactive Process Committee (Personal Records)

Dear Interactive Committee:

We are scheduled to meet on Thursday at one o'clock PM to discuss my accommodations. Because my plan is firmly on track, and because we are all very busy people, I'd like to suggest that we cancel our meeting. I provide the report below in lieu of our meeting.

My accommodations are working out quite well. It was initially difficult to obtain an assistant due to an apparent shortage of student workers at this time of the academic year. Ultimately, funds for an assistant were released to the department and I was able to select a person who I am comfortable with. I appreciate this added flexibility which allows me a much broader range of potential assistants.

My current assistant will graduate in May and I have begun searching for her replacement. In the meantime, she will continue to be especially helpful in monitoring weekly class attendance and communications, She has been of assistance by responding to routine email and phone messages, populating my new whiteboard with important dates, and helping to manage presentations, quizzes, and discussion boards. Short and long-range planning, organization of files, and project management activities will commence in May with the guidance of an Interwork staff member (who is known to be a master organizer).

For the current semester, we were unable to change the teaching schedule to reduce my late-night classes (7-9:40 PM) from two to one. For one of my two assigned late classes, I created a hybrid course, utilizing technology, which reduced the number of late-night meetings significantly. My department Chair has agreed to make any needed adjustment in my teaching schedule to limit my late-night classes to one per week in the future.

The accommodations provided through the university have already proved helpful, reducing my stress and my sense of being perpetually behind and/or missing important information/events. There is much to be done, however, and I am optimistic that the accommodations provided by the university will significantly ameliorate the symptoms of my disability.

Marjorie

# The Power Of Reasonable Accommodations

I semi-retired in 2019, making job accommodations no longer necessary. My most recent assistant, Karen, worked about 13 hours per week for me. She assisted with organizing tasks such as long-range planning, setting up meetings, planning and tracking projects, keeping lists of students and courses, and scheduling. In addition, she alerted me to any emails that need critical attention and reminded me of upcoming meetings and due dates. A skilled graphic designer and conceptual thinker, her help has been indispensable for large projects such as accreditation applications, brochure creation, writing tasks, and research. Beyond our professional relationship, we have become friends. A mother of a young man with a psychiatric disability and a graduate of our psychiatric rehabilitation program, I value her insights and enjoy our conversations. A lucky bonus!

But you have to wonder how my life might have been different if I had requested job accommodations early in my career. In terms of managing multiple priorities, the job would have been much less stressful. I may have been more productive, less symptomatic and far less stressed. However, the academic environment can be tricky. Until one gets tenure, the job is far from guaranteed. A faculty member's productivity is not the only variable that is being evaluated during the probationary period. I feared that colleagues would judge me to be less able if they knew I had a psychiatric disability. I worried that having accommodations might make colleague think that I had somehow "cheated" the system. Even after tenure and promotion to associate professor, I still had to prove my worth and my mental acuity. I considered asking for accommodations at that point but decided to postpone the request until the next (and final) promotion.

I don't recommend that others be so extremely cautious in pursuing job accommodations. I know from experience the value of a good accommodation and, in many ways, wish I hadn't been such a chicken. By law, employers must engage in the interactive process with an employee, seriously considering their request and providing a rationale if it is denied. They must be ready to suggest alternatives and assure that the plan is working by following up.

As discussed in the chapter on disclosure, deciding to request a job accommodation is individual, personal, and critical. Disclosing your disability to your boss or a trusted co-worker is qualitatively different from officially disclosing through human resources. However, in my experience, going through the interactive process and getting job accommodations that are both reasonable and effective, has been tremendously beneficial to me, my students, my department, and the university as a whole. I am much more productive and less likely to lose time due to psychiatric symptoms. I'm grateful for the ADA and job accommodations-- they have kept me productive and happily employed.

In evaluating the overall impact of having job accommodations, I would say that my productivity roughly doubled. The university got its money's-worth. For the small expense of $195 per week (13 hours per week times the graduate assistant rate of $15 per hour), I completed the following:

- Published nine articles
- Worked as an associate editor for a major journal
- Won four prestigious awards
- Procured 2.25 million dollars in grant monies
- Hosted a national conference
- Presented at eight local and national conferences
- Developed a graduate-level degree program
- Got the degree program officially accepted as for licensure in the State of California
- Procured nationally accredited for the new program
- Created an academic certificate program
- Created six new courses
- Chaired or served on 13 thesis and dissertation committees
- Taught 24 classes

Accommodations work. There is no way I could have accomplished all of these tasks in six years without help and support. They are cost-effective for companies because employees are more productive with accommodations than without them. They make for happier employers because employees are at their best most of the time instead of some of the time. Most of all, they take the stress off of employees with disabilities who know they can be productive at work "If only...." "If only" doesn't have to wait forever. Reasonable accommodations can mean the difference between stressing out and accomplishing little--and loving your job and accomplishing plenty!

### But Remember, Job Accommodations Can Be Tricky

Timing is everything when it comes to accommodations. Well, it's not everything, but the *when* is nearly as important as the *what* when it comes to asking for a reasonable accommodation under the ADA. Let's start with the *when*.

Should you disclose that you have a disability during the interview? I wouldn't. Even though the world is fairer and more tolerant toward people with disabilities than it once was, there is still some heavy stigma associated with psychiatric issues. What about in the first week? You might want your supervisor to see what you can do before asking for an accommodation. How about after the probationary period? Good idea! That timing is ideal because now everyone knows you are competent and capable, that you can fulfil the "essential functions" of the job. Moreover, you now know in what areas you might need accommodations.

What about the *what*? What accommodation, if any, are you going to need on the job, that's directly related to your disability, that everyone else doesn't automatically get? You might need breaks and an opportunity to take your medications on time. Labor laws are already on your side for these ones. You will get breaks every few hours and at least a half hour for lunch after you work a certain number of hours. No special accommodation is needed. What if you start the job and you are working in a noisy cubicle? Because of your disability, you're having a hard time concentrating. This one might require an accommodation, or maybe just earphones. Problem averted? Let's see. Being a proactive employee, you talk to your supervisor: "I'm finding it a bit noisy in here. Is it okay if I wear headphones?" If yes, you may not need any accommodation on this job. What if they reply "No. It's against company policy to use a headset"? *Now*, you may need an accommodation.

My first step in thinking about accommodations, way before actually asking for one, would be to do my research. In this case, I'm going to look into accommodations for concentration problems. "A website?" you ask. Yes, indeed. Go to the National Job Accommodation Network (JAN; www.askjan.org). JAN is an incredibly helpful site. All you need to do is to type in the name of your disability and possible accommodations pop up. When I search, I generally try an array of related disabilities. For example, for my own disability, bipolar disorder, I might also type in depression, schizophrenia, and ADHD as people with all of these disabilities may have trouble with concentration on the job. As you search, take notes on accommodations that might work for you. If you approach your employer asking for a reasonable accommodation, be aware that you'll need documentation of your disability and a fairly clear idea of what the accommodation should be. It's all in the homework (said the college professor).

Lesson Six: Reasonable accommodations can help you be more productive and happier at work. However, when requesting accommodations, it is as important when you ask as it is what you ask for. The interactive process requires disclosure, so that should be considered as well.

# LESSON SEVEN: WHAT COLOR IS MY WHAAT? CAREER EXPLORATION FOR THE 2020S

The last really big, important book on careers was *What Color is Your Parachute* by Richard N. Bolles. It was first published in (are you freaking kidding me?) 1970! As an economy, we sink billions into education and training every year, but hardly anyone really knows what they want to be when they grow up. In this lesson, I provide a history of my career, encourage you to develop your own work story, and provide information on how to figure out what you might want to do for a living. I also introduce the Social Security programs and provide some ideas on how to work when you are on benefits.

## A History Lesson

There are many resources and even some academic theories about how people end up in the jobs that they do. I doubt the value of some of what's out there, but, don't worry, I'll guide you to job resources that make sense. I start with my own career and a day that stands out in my memory, one that marks the beginning point of my psychiatric illness. I wrote the following journal entry when I first began writing the book. I just needed to get a sense for my beginnings.

## The Tipping Point (Journal Entry)

When experiencing a psychiatric crisis there may be no real beginning point, yet many of us remember the day we realized something had gone terribly wrong. For me, it was autumn 1984. I remember one afternoon clearly. As I stepped from my car—a bronze, 1970 Plymouth Valiant with a black rag roof, already an antique—the world was suddenly drained of color. I felt slow-churning nausea in the pit of my stomach and tasted metal on my tongue. The chrysanthemums on my walk, normally a deep, dusty red were gray. I panicked: *Something was not right.* I had a feeling of foreboding. I had been suspicious and anxious at work for months, now paranoia poured into my head in a gush: They *were* all talking about me. Just as I suspected! The world was not safe, and I needed to get into the house, into my bed. *Quickly.*

For over half my life, I have experienced the horror and despair that is depression as well as the high energy and sleepless nights associated with bipolar disorder. I have been plagued with frequent paranoid thoughts and have experienced auditory and visual hallucinations. I've even had periods of "mixed state" which combine the worst of both—the high energy of mania with the self-loathing, guilt, and distress of depression.

Although I had always experienced high and low moods, after that autumn day in 1984, I never functioned quite the same. I went through cycles of extreme energy and euphoria, anxiety and paranoia, and deep depression. On and off, I saw a therapist for my distress during these years, but refused to consider medication, even when the therapist who tried to convince me that there was a biological component to my feelings. I couldn't face the notion that my experiences were symptoms of an illness. Rather, I continued to think that my moods and thoughts were products of stress, or maybe childhood traumas I had yet to uncover.

This was my first mental health crisis of many. I was having unusual thoughts and visual distortions; however, I had no skills or knowledge to deal with what turned out to be months of acute distress. At the time, I literally believed that the fault was with my coworkers; I was not paranoid, they *were* all talking about me and that's why I felt the way I did. I never for a moment believed that something had changed in my head. Nor did I entertain the idea that I, personally, could get control of the feelings and "symptoms" and start recovering—if you don't own a problem, you're in no position to fix it. There is even a term for this; anosognosia: the lack of awareness of having a psychiatric disability. This complete unawareness is not the same as denial, where you have a glimmer of realization and are pushing that awareness away. Rather, it is interpreting any unusual behavior or experience as being external to you. The realization that there may be something "wrong with me" required both mounting evidence and a chink in the armor of my ego defenses.

I believe that many people with psychiatric and other disabilities are stuck in this place. For me, I didn't "own" my disability until ten years later when I finally agreed to take psychiatric medications and they helped. I made the connection between mood and drug, but not until there was biological evidence of a disorder—a pill helped me feel better. Better living through chemistry.

Having meaningful work has always been central to my identity and well-being, and it may be good for you as well. Interestingly, with all of its benefits, the least of which is a paycheck, people with psychiatric disabilities have often been discouraged from working by well-meaning clinicians. They have said that work is too stressful. The title of the following article should be a slogan on a t-shirt: "If work makes people with mental illness sick, what do unemployment, poverty, and social isolation cause?" In this vintage article, Marrone and Galowka (1999) discuss the benefits of work and make the case that in many cases, people with psychiatric disabilities can, should, and, most importantly, want to work. They are absolutely right: there is a body of research that shows the effectiveness of work in reducing symptoms of mental illness.

During my early career, I worked extensively with individuals with disabilities, assisting them to find employment that fit their skills, interests, and personalities. I took refuge in my work, using the structure and meaning as a sort of therapy. I did not always function at my very best, yet I was able to get myself to "suit up and show up," for the most part.

Prior to my doctoral work, my job required interfacing regularly with employers, negotiating the conditions of hiring, requesting accommodations, and working with co-workers on various job sites to create a comfortable work environment for a new employee with a disability. While helping people with disabilities to deal effectively with the business world, negotiate with employers, educate co-workers, and get accommodations, I struggled to maintain healthy relationships at work and keep my projects on track. I still had not made the connection between the needs of my clients for "reasonable accommodations" and my own, nor had it dawned on me that my feelings of alienation and paranoia within my own work team might be reduced through the use of some of the techniques that I was bringing to the workplaces of others. It was later that I started to put two and two together to make sense of my confusing situation.

## Doctoral Study

My commitment to helping people with disabilities gain full economic and social integration has been lifelong. In 1992, I returned to school for a doctorate to explore new ideas, strategies, and techniques. To reach this goal, I did not pursue a general human service degree such as psychology or social work, both excellent career paths for helping professionals. Instead, I matriculated in a doctoral program in rehabilitation counseling.

This lesser-known profession focuses exclusively on helping working-age adults with disabilities reach their goals—goals that include a gratifying career.

My four years of doctoral study were exciting and my mood climbed higher and higher by the month; I had a seemingly limitless capacity for work. I worked long hours, and eventually was sleeping only a couple of hours each night; this high energy state came at a price. I didn't realize it at the time, as my judgment was seriously impaired, but *I was experiencing a manic episode.*

The day I successfully defended my dissertation ended with a crippling, full-blown crash, falling from mania into a deep depression in a matter of hours. I now know to predict that after a major accomplishment I will invariably become depressed. It took me years to figure this out.

It was at this time that I first tried medication, and I came to this crossroads in an interesting way. I had discovered the attention deficit hyperactivity disorder (ADHD) diagnosis and thought it fit my high energy periods. Like so many people, I just could not accept the idea that I had a mental illness and this less stigmatizing disorder, ADHD, was acceptable to me. In my mind, I was simply hyperactive, inattentive, overworked and surrounded by people who apparently spent all their free time talking about me. In Lesson 4, I discussed my journey with medication in depth; here, let me tell you the story of Dexadrine and how I got my hands on it.

## My Introduction to Psychiatry

Before defending my dissertation and many times since, I have experienced manic episodes—little sleep, poor judgment, grandiose plans, intense levels of activity, and lots of pressured talking. I did not know that mania was a "thing" at the time, but I was desperate for solutions to my distress. After a short search, I found the name of a psychiatrist who treated ADHD and made an appointment. I said to him, "Doc, I can't stop talking and I can't sit in a chair. I feel like ants are crawling around in my brain." He diagnosed me with ADHD and prescribed Ritalin.

When I reported back to him that I continued to be revved up but that Ritalin, paradoxically, made me fall asleep at the wheel, he prescribed Dexadrine, basically, speed. In retrospect, I may have been falling asleep while driving because I had been manic for weeks, sleeping only one or two hours per night. Honestly, being a true child of the 60s, I liked the Dexadrine and went back for refills. I was still manic and now energized by a powerful drug.

You see the critical importance of finding a psychiatrist who will objectively and carefully evaluate and diagnose? Who does not have a specific bias? In this case, seeking the counsel of a psychiatrist who specialized in ADHD led to an ADHD diagnosis and treatment. Even though I presented with a textbook case of mania, he was looking for ADHD and that's what he found.

**The Path to Destruction**

I tried working during this time and was fired from not one, but two jobs. My judgment was seriously impaired by the mania, and I was working around the clock, developing proposals and instigating new plans, all without the approval of my supervisor. My supervisor, at her wits end, insisted that I go to the Employee Assistance Program (EAP) counselor to get help for my work problems. The therapist rapidly diagnosed me with bipolar disorder and I was incensed! I absolutely rejected the diagnosis as it was just too scary to think about. I did seek the assistance of a new psychiatrist when I again became depressed. She prescribed Wellbutrin, an antidepressant, but never asked about symptoms of mania. To be fair, I went to see her when I was depressed, never thinking to describe the manic episodes because I didn't know what they were. Also, to be equally fair, she should have asked.

Within weeks following the second firing, Sharon was diagnosed with Hodgkin's Disease, a form of lymphoma. I cared for my partner during a year of chemotherapy, radiation, and hospitalizations. Our cat was part of the team, making sure that some part of her was touching Sharon at all times, whether it be just the tip of her tail or the full weight of her little body. She seemed to know she was on the healing team. What I did during this difficult year was to read book after book to Sharon as she was too weak to hold a book and too tired to focus (yes, the kitty was there, but I wouldn't give her a quiz if I were you). My experience as a caregiver was sobering and, in a way, grounding. Sharon, fortunately, fully recovered. *I did not.*

By 1997, I was stable enough to procure a tenure-track faculty position at a Midwest university. Sharon, although still weak, agreed to the move, and sustained by a wish, a prayer, and Wellbutrin, we moved far away from our close circle of family and friends. As my symptoms worsened, I hung in there-- teaching courses, conducting research, and writing articles-- through periods of crippling mania, anxiety, depression, and paranoia. Looking back, it was actually the mania and one very special colleague, Nyna, that got me through. Conversations with my friend grounded me and, on more than one occasion, she was there to help in a crisis. Creative and productive periods offset the near paralysis of depression and Nyna was always the voice of reason.

It was a psychiatrist in Illinois who provided me with an accurate diagnosis of bipolar disorder and the corresponding treatment. This time, I was able to hear the diagnosis and internalize it. I had taken the over-the-counter remedy Sam-E to see if it would help with my feelings of depression. Within a half-hour, I was fully manic. When Sharon read the fine print on the bottle, she noted that it clearly stated that the supplement not be taken by individuals with bipolar disorder. I can see why! I saw my psychiatrist immediately and she prescribed lithium. Lithium was a revelation: It normalized my mood within just a few days. Between my first episode and finally accepting my diagnosis, 13 years had elapsed.

**The Silver Lining**

Although there are some difficult aspects of my life and career, I don't want to focus on the negative. I approach my life with humor and grace, for the most part. Moreover, the lessons learned have served me well. Through work, love, friendships, graduate study, and an academic career, I have amassed some very useful knowledge and a great deal of wisdom. My experiences taught me what I need for career success and what kinds of situations trip me up.

In the years since my most recent crisis, four decades since my original breakdown, I still experience withering dips into depression and expansive moods, high, restless energy, followed by sleeplessness and paranoia. My mood disorder has been partially controlled through medication and therapy, job accommodations, environmental adaptation, and healthy self-talk over the years, yet, it is still my nemesis, always lurking in the corner of my conscious awareness, always a challenge to my job performance.

Now that you have a window into my job experience, perhaps you'll write about your own. Let your imagination run wild as you think of possible future careers. Spend some time thinking about what you really enjoyed doing in the past and ways you might have more of this kind of work in the future—and get paid for it, of course. Life is rich and there is much to be gained by taking risks and trying new things.

## Getting From Here To There: How To Plan A Career

It may look like we're making a giant leap from my career history to planning a career of your own, but I'm talking about you getting what you want, and I'm guessing one of those things is a great job. Getting into that career you have always dreamt of doesn't need to stay in the realm of dreams forever. One of the best kept secrets in the United States is the state-federal vocational rehabilitation system. Every state and territory has a vocational rehabilitation department, funded by federal and state monies, that provides—and pays for—education and training leading to the career of your choice. I know, this sounds too good to be true, but it isn't. To find the vocational rehabilitation department in your location, go to this website: https://rsa.ed.gov/about/states. Vocational rehabilitation services are for people who have documented disabilities and can include a huge array of benefits including computer equipment, tuition, fees, and books for college programs, training in the trades, self-employment, and so many other benefits. If you are unemployed, living on Social Security, or working in an entry-level job that is not a dream career, vocational rehabilitation might be your ticket to a rewarding and satisfying career.

Okay, okay...you may have heard horror stories from friends and family members about state vocational rehabilitation. It's true, these are big, impersonal bureaucracies that make you feel like a number, but this chapter is about focusing on what *you* want out of life and how you can get it. I'm talking about free education and training and so much more. Isn't that worth a little bureaucracy? *Do* look into vocational rehabilitation and *do* apply. *Do* jump through a few hoops and use your skills and knowledge to get the education and training you have always wanted.

Here's what you can expect when you contact your state vocational rehabilitation office. Once you apply for vocational rehabilitation services, you may be asked to attend a group orientation. Later, a counselor will conduct an "intake," gathering documentation on your disability or referring you for evaluation. People are accepted for services when they meet the criterion of having a serious disability, and most psychiatric disabilities fall into this category. Once accepted for services, you and your counselor will develop what is called an "Individualized Plan for Employment" or IPE. This plan is a collaborative agreement that is ideally developed with two experts in the room: your counselor who is a vocational rehabilitation expert, and you, an expert on your life and career. The IPE is essentially a contract between you and your counselor (and your state vocational rehabilitation agency) for future services leading to your new career, so it is very important. Take your time when constructing your IPE, just as you would any other contractual agreement.

### Judy's New Career (case study)

I want to illustrate vocational rehabilitation services using a case study. Let's say Judy, who is diagnosed with clinical depression, has always wanted to be a middle school science teacher (God love her!) but she only has a high school degree. She'll need a master's degree and a teaching credential to reach her goal. Judy's IPE plan might include:

- A laptop computer
- Internet service
- Money for travel
- Two years of tuition, books, and fees at her local community college resulting in a degree in Humanities
- Two years of tuition, fees, and books at her local four-year university leading to a degree in Liberal Arts
- Two years of tuition, fees, and books at the university leading to a master's degree in Education and her coveted teaching credential
- Assistance with the job search process

That's three degrees cooler, six years of funding richer, and a shiny new career for Judy. And, the plan could contain other services, depending on Judy's individual situation and needs.

With vocational rehabilitation, your counselor not only provides the services included in the IPE, rehabilitation counselors are trained to provide counseling in all areas related to career preparation and career success. A word of warning: you'll have to brush off your people skills to navigate the labyrinth that is state vocational rehabilitation. Things may not go as planned, there may be red tape, but always think to yourself "What do *I* want." If you keep your goals at the center of your planning and actions, you'll be more skillful in your interactions with the people who can help you realize your goal. One additional piece of information about state-federal vocational rehabilitation: if you run into a snag or come up against too many "no's," don't give up. The system has its own problem solvers who will work with you to get to "yes." These folks are affiliated with the Client Assistance Program, or CAP. Find your CAP representative through your vocational rehabilitation provider and let them help you though the red tape.

Going to state vocational rehabilitation is a smart move if you know what you want to be or do. Many people are not sure what they would like, or what kind of job they would be good at. This next section addresses choosing a career.

## But I Don't Know What I Want To Do!

We don't all come into this world knowing what we want to be when we grow up. As a society, we don't even talk about this very important aspect of life very much. As a rehabilitation counselor educator, I have a few resources for you to check out if you need to explore possible careers, figure out what career might be right for you, or both.

A cool resource for exploring possible careers is O*NET (https://www.onetonline.org/). This website provides exhaustive data on almost any career you can think of. Using this database, you can find out what the job prospects are for any given career in your state and what the beginning and average salaries are. You can even see whether people are hiring for the jobs you like, and find jobs that are similar to your favorites if they are not. You can also do some self-assessment to see what your skills are in various areas and even what you might be interested in.

If you're not sure what you want to do, I suggest you complete an interest inventory online to discover where your interests fall. Interests in the "Holland" categories include the following broad categories: realistic, investigatory, conventional, artistic, social, enterprising, or investigatory. The website (https://www.hollandcodes.com/) provides an interesting tool to help you to clarify for yourself the kinds of activities you like and, more importantly, the job tasks that would be deadly boring or distasteful for you. Besides, learning more about yourself and your interests is a fun way to while away a lazy Sunday afternoon. That's what I did. I wasn't surprised to learn that I am investigative and social. Yup, I'm a researcher and an educator, so my career has been a good fit. Didn't need an interest inventory to figure that out, but the confirmation is nice!

## Let's Skip the Career Development Theories

There are several theories about how people select their career path but the theories are old and mostly outdated. Actually, Holland (who you met above) is the author of one of the theories, so you already know a bit about one of them. Let me tell you, though, about why I don't give these crusty old theories any credence. Primarily, the theories were developed before being a woman in the workplace was accepted as a normal part of life. In addition, the theories were created without any thought to how these theoretical constructs would fit people of color. I'm not saying that women and people of color were not in the workplace—they most certainly were. It's just that their experience was largely excluded from the theories. I know, hard to believe, huh? Early career development theories were based on white, middle class, educated men's careers, excluding women (who often have unique trajectories as people who can give birth and are usually the primary parents to infants and children), as well as the rich but often fraught experience of people of color. Another problem with early theories is that they viewed careers as relatively static. Especially in today's job market, careers are dynamic, people change jobs and fields readily, and traditional boss-employee roles have been superseded by contract work, gig work, or self-employment.

I hope you are not sad about missing out on a few dry theories. I seriously considered adding them, just to be thorough, but you now know what you need to know. You're entering a dynamic and exciting, sometimes confusing, job environment. Within that community, you will express certain gifts and abilities on the job while learning to avoid things that simply don't interest you. Your own career goals may change over time as you accrue more job experience, or you may find that you have a very good idea of what you want to do for work.

## So-So Security: Not So Hot

Social Security Disability Insurance (SSDI) and Supplemental Security Income (SSI), both administered by the Social Security Administration, can be helpful programs when you need maintenance income and health insurance to get through a crisis. You pay into SSDI through your FICA taxes (take a look at a paycheck to see). Therefore, people who have worked a certain number of quarters are eligible for SSDI and Medicare. Those without a work history or with a very short work history are eligible for SSI and Medicaid.

Both of these programs can also make it very hard for you to get back into the world of work. I spent 15 years researching the work incentive programs (and perhaps more importantly, the *disincentives* to employment) provided by the Social Security Administration and I can tell you without a doubt that these programs are like Roach Motel—you can get in, but you don't come back out.

Why is it so hard to return to work after getting benefits? Unfortunately, it comes down to the definition of disability that the Social Security uses to determine eligibility. An applicant needs to be unable to do any "substantial gainful activity" (a dollar amount that increases slightly each year) in order to qualify. Even though Social Security has developed several work incentive programs over the years, returning to work when on benefits can be daunting. For example, people on SSDI can earn above the level of substantial gainful activity for nine months while still receiving their SSDI check. After that, Social Security drops them like a hot potato. Both the monthly checks and the Medicare stop. Those on SSI have it a little easier. After a certain amount of wages, SSI will deduct a dollar from your SSI check for every two dollars you earn and you keep your Medicaid. Under the SSI rules, you always do a little better when you work whereas on SSDI it's all or nothing.

There are several factors that mitigate against employment for Social Security recipients. First, just getting on benefits can be a years-long process of working through red tape, hearings, denials, and reapplications. It's so hard to get on that people can't imagine voluntarily giving up the benefits. Second, the rules that govern Social Security programs and work are extensive and not easy to understand. Few people feel secure enough in their ability to comprehend bureaucracy-speak to risk making one wrong move. Third, there is often a niggling fear that you'll need benefits down the road. If you go off benefits today, what happens tomorrow if you get really sick?

Understanding the disincentive to employment endemic to the Social Security programs, how can we move forward toward that career of our dreams. Working with some colleagues, I did an interview study of 22 people who had successfully gotten off benefits and back into the workforce (Olney, et al., 2014). What they said was enlightening. It turns out that strong role modeling, parental encouragement, and *pressure from parents* were the factors that were most influential in helping the study participants toward a career. Additional factors were mentoring by respected peers and support from vocational rehabilitation counselors. Although getting off benefits was still quite difficult, helpful factors went a long way toward helping individuals make the leap from living on SSDI or SSI to remunerative employment. In other words, a combination of high expectations and excellent support were the most helpful. I suggest that, if you are on benefits and you'd like to get back to work, you learn all you can about the Social Security work incentive programs. For that you'll need another online resource. The Red Book (https://www.ssa.gov/redbook/) provides detailed information about the SSDI and SSI loopholes that will help you keep some or all of your benefits while trying your hand at work.

Lastly, for most people with disabilities, it is the health insurance that comes along with SSI and SSDI that is most important. The monthly check is secondary. There are work incentive programs that will keep you on your benefits for months, sometimes years, but not forever. For those who are on SSDI consider the Affordable Care Act (ACA) to replace your Medicare. There is no national website for the ACA, so search ACA and the name of your state for information on this healthcare option. The ACA is subsidized, so the monthly premiums are low when your monthly income is low, and higher when your income goes up.

Yes, Social Security does pose a barrier to employment, but it is not insurmountable. Between the work incentive programs (found in the Red Book) and the ACA, you have a safety net that will allow you to try working. One final comment on Social Security: in my research, I also discovered that people make rational decisions about their benefits and employment. I'll let Richard explain.

## Richard Returns To Work (Case Study)

In this case, we'll say that Richard is currently on SSDI and is looking to try to return to his former career as an engineer. Richard might consider returning to work if the job meets his needs:

- Is the job full time? Does it come with health insurance benefits? If so, Richard will likely take the job. If not, he might evaluate whether the pay level can afford him insurance, in which case, he might take the job.
- Is the job part-time? Does it come with health insurance benefits? If the job is part time with benefits, Richard might take the job. If it doesn't have health benefits, Richard will evaluate whether the wages are low enough for him to keep his SSDI and Medicare. If either of these conditions are met, he might take the job (Olney, 2007).

Richard is a person and people are rational. They usually consider their best interests, and decisions about Social Security and employment are no exception. It is possible to make the leap to employment from benefits, but I would be lying if I said it was easy.

Being on Social Security benefits does not preclude work. Admittedly, being on benefits does complicate the process. On one side of the equation, getting a (usually small) monthly check and health insurance benefits provide the safety net you need, or needed at some point in your life. On the other side, the world of work offers much better pay, often medical benefits, a chance to build your skills and competencies, opportunities for new friendships, intellectual challenges, often retirement benefits, and many intangible rewards. I invite you to weigh the pros and cons and I'm confident that you will choose work. After all, it is the best medicine!

Lesson Seven: Building the career you want is possible and the multitude of resources available make it more manageable than ever. Even if you are on Social Security benefits, you can have a rewarding career.

# LESSON EIGHT: "GET A JOB" SURE. BUT WHAT DO I DO ONCE I GET IT?

After a lifetime of successful employment, helping people get jobs, and teaching others how to do that, I'm excited to share what I know about how to succeed on the job. In this lesson, I cover one critical issue: how to succeed, advance, and thrive in your job by developing the soft skills you will need to get along with supervisors and coworkers. You may not think this is very imperative, but this lesson might be the most important one in the book.

As you know by now, the thread that runs through this book, implicitly or explicitly, is how to succeed in employment. Throughout the book, I explored my own experiences related to work—how I managed my symptoms so that I could be successful at work, how I negotiated job accommodations, the pros and cons of disclosure at work, and methods for managing medications so that I *can* work—to provide a model for how you can be successful in your career.

One thing I have learned in my life and career: A substantial limitation need not be a permanent barrier to employment. I have a legally blind cousin who needs specialized computer equipment at work that magnifies his font to 90-point type so that he can read his screen. As discussed in Lesson 6, reasonable accommodations in the workplace are guaranteed under the Americans with Disabilities Act (ADA). However, an employee with a disability needs to be savvy about how to determine what might work, how to ask for it, and the limits of the protections under the law. We all need to attend to issues of disclosure, documentation, formal and informal supports, and other factors related to accommodations. We all need the resources, knowledge, and skills to embark on a career, find the work we love, and become a success, however we come to define it.

## Skillful Means, Anyone?

I'd like to jump right in with a lesson on how to stay employed once you get that coveted job. We've covered a lot of concepts, so why not examine what a Buddhist might do in the workplace. I start specifically with the Buddhist concept of skillful means: The skills, abilities, and attitudes that get you where you want to go while leaving other people and the environment relatively unscathed. These skills are a part of what are often called "soft skills" in the world of business, but they also go beyond soft skills to introduce compassion and understanding for our coworkers and supervisors. Brightwayzen.org/ describes the nuances of skillful means as follows:

> ...even if we possess wisdom, when we want to share it with other beings and help them...we need to be patient, creative, and compassionate so they will be able to hear, accept, and act on what we have to share.

I am amazed at how often I need to get out and brush off the "skillfuls" in a typical week at the office, not just for me, but for people around me as well. Because my symptoms sometimes make it hard for me to readily interpret people's behaviors, I watch people carefully so that I can determine what their thoughts and goals are. That way I'll know how to respond.

Interactions in the workplace often seemed mysterious to me over the years, and if you have a psychiatric disability, they may seem foreign or illogical to you as well. One thing I have learned through a lifetime of studying work is that workplace behaviors are generally goal-oriented. The goals of individual workers can run counter to the goals of the organization and they are often self-centered. However, they are rarely irrational. So, I invite you to "strap on a pair of skillfuls" and explore functional and dysfunctional behaviors at work with me.

Here I provide two case studies, both hypothetical, to illustrate skillful means.

## Marissa And Toby React Badly (Case Studies)

Here is the first scenario:

A young woman, a student we'll call Marissa, comes to me to talk about a conflict she is having in her job as a human services worker. She has decided that management is acting in an unethical way toward the clients and has decided to skip up the chain of command (her supervisor, her supervisor's supervisor, etc.) to report the perceived infraction to the corporate office. In this scenario, Marissa is both distressed and indignant (which can be a lethal combination of emotions on the job). I quickly surmise that she has decided on a course of action that will ultimately hurt her both in this job and in her career.

Here is a second scenario:

My fellow committee member, who we'll call Toby, sits down in my office with fire in his eyes and fury on his face. He announces heatedly that our college's representative, Ellen, has complained about the way our committee is managing our work. Apparently, Ellen thinks that our committee is not being thorough enough in evaluating some of the proposals, and she shared this opinion. I have no doubts that Toby's angry voice is going to result in angry and unproductive behavior toward Ellen.

Let's take the first example: What will happen if Marissa follows through on her impulse to skip the chain of command

and go to corporate? I can guarantee that there will be ruffled feathers all the way up and down that chain! The problem, in management's mind, will be resolved when the young employee is removed from her job. It may not happen immediately, but everyone along that chain will be looking for just the right opportunity. Skipping the chain of command sets off a psychological siren within an organization that reverberates for years. In other words, it's not a skillful move. Only if Marissa's goal is to never work for this organization again does her action makes sense. If her goal, on the other hand, is advocating for her clients to make sure they are treated fairly and equitably, she had better find a more skillful way to respond. And what would be the skillful means of response?

First of all, I ask, what does Marissa want? She tells me that she wants to be an advocate for people with disabilities. She wants to change what she sees as an uncaring and unresponsive system to one that truly puts the clients first. She wants to eventually be promoted in the organization where she can really do some good. Five years down the road, she sees herself as a community leader. With these goals in mind, should her first stop be the corporate offices, complaining loudly to the vice president of clinical services? I think not. To start, I suggest that she immediately stop complaining about the situation to all who have ears. Organizations value employees with tact, good judgment, and self-control.

Marissa then needs to disengage from the idea that going to corporate is the only strong response she can make and develop a new plan that will be appropriate, effective, and, well, skillful. I would encourage Marissa to write down the facts of the situation she observed—documentation is important. A logical next step might be to make an appointment with her supervisor, sharing her observation, reporting the situation as she sees it, honestly and calmly, and seeking advice. She might set up a follow-up meeting with the supervisor to discuss outcomes as well. This mindful action will result in Marissa being both responsible and responsive while skillfully working toward her goals of advancement and success in her career.

One more thing about Marissa's situation. In my job as a college professor, I deal with young people all the time. One beautiful thing about youth is idealism. But this very trait that helps us grow into sensitive, caring, and effective adults can be a stumbling block in those early days at work, especially when the idealism turns into self-righteousness. I see this all of the time: one event can spark angry conversations, bad energy, and a work environment that doesn't "work" for anyone. I wish I could say that I've been able to dissuade young people from such unskillful actions, but my sober advice is rarely heeded. I'm hoping that you, on the other hand, will see this lesson for what it is, a lesson to help you respond with more skill and greater insight on the job.

How about my colleague, Toby? What are his goals in this situation? To be fair, Toby wants and needs to feel respected, and Ellen's actions undermined those needs. By voicing her concerns publicly, Ellen put both Toby and myself in a difficult situation. Hey, I'm part of this as well. As Toby's coworker, what are my goals? As the third person in this triad, my goal is to do excellent committee work, and Ellen's action provided a great opportunity to potentially fix what I hadn't realized was broken. In terms of skillful means, Ellen could and should have come to us with her concerns rather than raising them in a meeting. But no matter.

While sitting with me in my office, Toby fumed for a few minutes when I interrupted him with "I have an idea. I'm going to make Ellen my best friend." Toby was more than a little skeptical about my plan. Actually, he was flabbergasted.

I did schedule a meeting with Ellen in that same week. Toby didn't want to go with me, so I met with Ellen myself. I shared with her how we were conducting our committee reviews and asked her for feedback about what would be most helpful to her as our college representative. I never confronted her about publicly saying negative things about how we were managing proposals or not coming to us first. That would have put her on the defensive and my goal was to make Ellen my ally. I

MARJORIE F. OLNEY PH.D.

did finish the meeting with gratitude for sharing her knowledge and with the promise that I would continue to seek her out to discuss our mutual interests and concerns. I made Ellen my best friend and we never heard another word of complaint. To this day, I have a great relationship with Ellen and with Toby (although I don't think they speak to each other).

So being skillful at work starts with a goal. What do I want to accomplish here? How do I want the situation to look when I'm done? Being skillful in your behavior and communication does not mean you need to shut up or play dead. It does, however, mean that you approach a potentially dangerous (to you) situation with reasonable caution.

### Put the Small "p" in Politics

We generally think of politics as contests that happen at the local, state, and national levels. The political arena is characterized by a contest of ideas and values, often played out in a dirty way with a "winner takes all" mentality. Politics go on in the office as well. They comprise all the little contests and conflicts that happen every day at work and in life, and the helpful and harmful ways players in the environment respond to them. How you deal with these little landmines will help to determine your success on the job. Using the framework of skillful means, you want to think carefully about the outcomes you hope to see for yourself and others. For example, being "political" at work means having insight about how a supervisor is going to feel or react if you are chronically late for work and knowing how to correct the problem by both taking responsibility for the behavior and taking the initiative to change it. Being "political" helps you to figure out what to do and say if and when coworkers become jealous that you got a job accommodation and they didn't (yes, I know they don't *need* the accommodation, but jealousy doesn't need to make sense). Skillful means and thinking politically give you the ability to talk to your supervisor when something goes wrong, listen to your supervisor when they have a problem with you or your performance, and articulate your plan of correction both when you are in the wrong and when you'd like to see something changed.

Lesson Eight rounds out our discussion of skillful means. I think employers do want employees with the job skills that are required, sure they do. But much more than that, employers deeply value employees who are mature, discrete, thoughtful in their words and actions, and prepared. As you re-enter the world of work, bring your best self. Avoid the gossip and the divisive behavior. Carry yourself like the fine Buddhist I know you can be.

# LESSON NINE: THE ALPHABET SOUP OF HELPFUL STRATEGIES

We just had two lessons about developing a career; first, my job experience, career strategies and resources; second, skillful means. Here we make an abrupt u-turn from the world of work to the world inside as we address the critical issue of support. Lessons 9, 10, and 11 deal with how to get the most out of therapy, how to identify the right professional help, and the importance of informal support. You'll readily recognize the connections between appropriate support and success on the job.

There is probably a ton of information about strategies that you can use, by yourself or with a therapist, to stay well; methods that will help you get and stay happy, healthy, and employed. I've already talked about WRAP, a strategy that helps you manage your symptoms, day-by-day and hour-by-hour. Here, I introduce two different, but equally powerful methods that you can use, either with a therapist or on your own: cognitive behavioral therapy (CBT) and motivational interviewing (MI). CBT is a set of approaches that helps you counter your own negative and unhelpful thoughts. MI employs a variety of methods to prepare you to make a major change in your life like quitting smoking or returning to work. It is quite different from CBT and focuses on ambivalence--feeling two ways about something. You might ask, "When do I feel two ways about something?" Generally, people feel ambivalent when an issue is vitally important to them and they are about to embark on a change related to that issue. A classic case would be considering ending or changing a long-term relationship or quitting smoking. Only resolving the ambivalence about the upcoming change will allow you to embark on a new way of life. CBT and MI, singly or combined, can equip you with multiple options when you hit a snag.

It has become apparent to me over the years that succeeding in a career takes much more than simply being assigned tasks I can do, an understanding boss, and job accommodations. In addition to these things I have to consider my symptoms and balance my state of mind with my responsibilities. Some, maybe most, people with psychiatric disabilities need to actively monitor their symptoms and take appropriate action to manage them. It's important to have good strategies in addition to support and accommodations, and I can't think of better ones than CBT and MI, both proven by research to be effective for helping people manage their symptoms.

Strategies for managing various states of mind are highly individualized, requiring approaches that are flexible and powerful. What can we do if we have a touchy psychological system? I recommend the following goals, and a good CBT or MI therapist would as well: (1) Reduce the stress in your life by managing your environment; (2) Reduce symptoms such as anxiety, depression, mania, psychosis, withdrawal, and agitation using strategies that have proven effective; and (3) Improve integration and functioning by using strategies that help to keep you well. If you have read this book up to this chapter, you already have a broad range of skills to help you accomplish all three. Using CBT and MI, with a therapist or by employing self-help strategies using a workbook or guide, can help make these goals second nature.

## What Is Cognitive Behavioral Therapy?

CBT is a therapeutic approach to managing thoughts and emotions that are (a) unhelpful; (b) cause distress; and (c) many times irrational. It is based on several principles that are easy to understand:

- Your thoughts, feelings, and behaviors are all connected
- Thoughts precede feelings--and impact behavior
- Recognizing and identifying unhelpful thoughts are the first steps in CBT
- You can learn to recognize and change unhelpful thoughts and beliefs
- Addressing specific thoughts in reaction to certain situations allows you to correct those thoughts and avoid the bad feelings that come with bad thoughts
- You can manage unhelpful thoughts and develop more realistic cognitions

Wright and his colleagues (2009) cite research that shows that CBT is effective for serious disabilities such as clinical depression, bipolar disorder, schizoaffective disorder (that combines mood disorder and schizophrenia), and schizophrenia. There is plenty of scientific evidence that CBT is helpful to all of us, and it is clearly the right choice for people with psychiatric disabilities.

On page 50 of *Ten Days to Self*-Esteem, an excellent CBT workbook that I recommend, David Burn (1999) identifies the unhelpful thoughts that often accompany emotional distress as follows:

1. All or nothing thinking: You look at things in absolute, black or white categories.

2. Overgeneralization: You view a negative event as a never-ending pattern of defeat.

3. Mental filter: You dwell on the negatives and ignore the positives.

4. Discounting the positives: You insist that your accomplishments or positive qualities don't count.

5. Jumping to conclusions: You conclude things are bad without any definite evidence.

(a)     Mind reading: You assume people are reacting negatively to you.

(b)     Fortune-telling: You predict things will turn out badly.

6. Magnification and minimization: You blow things way out of proportion or you shrink their importance.

7. Emotional reasoning: You reason from how you feel: "I feel like an idiot, so I must be one."

8. "Should" statements: You criticize yourself or other people with "shoulds," "shouldn'ts," "musts," "oughts," and "have-tos."

9. Labeling: Instead of saying, "I made a mistake," you tell yourself, "I'm a jerk" or "a loser."

10. Blame: You blame yourself for something you weren't entirely responsible for, or you blame other people and overlook ways that you contributed to the problem.

Do any of these seem familiar to you? I don't know about you, but I engage in all of these unhelpful ways of thinking in the course of any given week. These are exactly the kinds of unhelpful thoughts that you can modify with CBT. I can tell you from experience that I can reduce my level of distress in just a few minutes by identifying the unhelpful thought and refuting it.

**CBT Techniques**

Cognitive behavioral therapists draw on an assortment of techniques to help you get a better grasp on your thoughts and emotions. Here are three of the most popular interventions:

Socratic Questioning: Asking logical questions to gently help someone determine if his or her hypothesis is correct. Rather than challenge your beliefs directly, the cognitive behavior therapist will help you to identify unhelpful thoughts through subtle yet specific lines of questioning. For example, the counselor might ask "I wonder what evidence there is to support the idea that your coworkers hate you?"

Reality Testing: Examining the evidence for and against a belief. Again, the cognitive behavior therapist will encourage you to identify factors that both refute and support an unhelpful belief. They may assign homework to teach you how to do this for yourself. For example, to help a person who thinks the government is spying on him through the heat vents in his apartment, the counselor might suggest that the person examine the vents to see if there are spying devices hidden there.

Mindfulness: Various forms of meditation help a person focus on the current moment. The cognitive behavior therapist provides a variety of options for relaxation and mindfulness. This technique, when learned, will provide you with the mental space to examine unhelpful thoughts and reactions. For example, the counselor might teach relaxation exercises that can be used in stressful moments. (Pratt, et al., 2014)

Using CBT might look something like this: first, identify the irrational or unhelpful thoughts. In my case, the thought might be "People are judging me negatively." Second, identify a positive thought to explain the situation such as "People make all kinds of faces. They don't necessary mean anything negative." Third, substitute the rational thought for the irrational or unhelpful one. "The evidence indicates that everyone likes me just fine." Simple as that! Many people find it useful to do this renaming using pen and paper. Seeing the words can help to reinforce new learning.

**The Assessment Process**

Based on an interview, the cognitive behavior therapist will pull together your concerns, your goals, and your needs, making a plan for future sessions. The therapist may take biological, psychological, and social aspects into account, personalizing your plan, considering all aspects of your life to assess the factors that both cause you difficulty and what will help in the recovery process: (1) Historical and current situations that predispose you to unhelpful thoughts and feelings; (2) Precipitating factors that have caused your current distress; (3) Factors that tend to perpetuate unhelpful cognitions; and (4) Protective factors that encourage helpful cognitions. The therapist may evaluate your mental state each time they see you by examining factors that impede or encourage your happiness and stability: thoughts, feelings, body sensations, and behaviors.

**Getting Professional Help**

Although there are great self-help books that teach you how to use CBT, such as the one by David Burn, I would suggest that you start with a cognitive behavioral therapist. I learned and practiced CBT with a trained therapist for a year. In addition to weekly sessions, homework assignments, and working through a workbook, we examined the distressing and paranoid thoughts that haunted me, especially when I was feeling depressed. I have never completely eradicated my tendency to "jump to conclusions" that people are talking about me or "discount the positives" when there is evidence that people have a favorable view of me, but I now have specific tools that I use to address the overwhelming emotions that accompany my negative thoughts.

# What Is Motivational Interviewing?

I wrote about things that make me feel ambivalent such as navigating relationships when I perceive that I am being judged, and maintaining my equilibrium in unstructured social situations. Ambivalence makes it impossible to plan or move forward, and the more important the situation is, the more ambivalent you will feel. What if I told you I know a method for resolving ambivalence? Happily, I do. Nearly 40 years ago, William Miller and Stephen Rollnick developed motivational interviewing (MI), a brief, collaborative counseling style that helps people make changes in their lives by exploring and resolving ambivalence: feeling two ways about behavior change.

It began as a method to help problem drinkers but, after successful implementation with this population, was expanded to help with any desired behavior change (Miller & Rollnick, 2013). Whereas CBT provides strategies for managing unhelpful thoughts and feelings on a day-to-day basis, MI is most useful for developing a plan of action for behavior change. Many therapists will use MI to help their clients commit to a plan, then turn to CBT strategies to supplement the MI process of implementing the plan, using MI and CBT in tandem.

Miller and Rollnick (2013) describe motivation as something that everyone has. But we are often motivated in two directions: to maintain the status quo or make a change. Often, people feel two ways about change: on one hand, they want something different; on the other hand, they are used to their current state of being and are drawn to the status quo. One of the underlying foundations of MI is the six stages of change: precontemplation, contemplation, preparation, action, maintenance, and setback/relapse (Prochaska & DiClemente, 1982). The stages of change were not developed by Rollnick and Miller, but they provide a useful framework for understanding the way people address change in their everyday lives.

## Andre Makes A Choice (Case Study)

Here, rather than using myself as an example, I'd like to introduce the stages using the hypothetical case of Andre. Let's say he is a young guy in his late 20s who has been on SSI benefits for the past two years but often thinks he would like to work. He is ambivalent because he is afraid that if he works he will lose his Social Security benefits. At the same time, he is bored, tired of living on the tiny income he gets from the federal government, and ready to use the bachelor's degree in business that he earned before he became ill with schizophrenia. Depending on what stage of change Andre is experiencing, he will say and do specific things that indicate his state of mind. The MI counselor listens carefully to assess what stage of change Andre is in, calibrating their responses to Andre in a way that meets him exactly where he is at the time. I have provided an example of what Andre might sound like if he were in each of the stages of change.

1. **Precontemplation**. If he is precontemplative, Andre does not see the need for change. Precontemplation could sound like this: "I'm fine the way I am. I don't want to think about getting a job right now. Besides, I know I can count on my SSI check."

2. **Contemplation**: In this stage of change, Andre is just beginning to desire change or think about a need for a change. In no way is he ready to take the leap. Contemplation might sound like this: "I'd like to work and earn more money but this is not the right time. Maybe I'll work on this next year. I'd really like to do something but I'm afraid of losing my benefits"

3. **Preparation**. This stage begins when the person is beginning to seriously consider a change. In Andre's case, preparation might sound like this: "I really want to use my degree and get a great job. I'll look into getting some help from state vocational rehabilitation this week."

4. **Action**. Action is taking steps toward change. In the action phase, Andre might say one of the following statements; "I met with my vocational rehabilitation counselor this week. I've decided to start looking for a job." "My symptoms have been pretty well-controlled and my strategies are working really well. I'm sure I can meet my goal of working."

5. **Maintenance**. In this stage, a person has met their goal but needs to sustain their success over time. Andre might say something like this: "My new job at the insurance company is going well and I think I can do this long-term. I have passed my probationary period at work and have been thinking about what I might do to get promoted" or

> "I've learned so much about this, I could write a book!"
> 6. **Setback**. Setbacks are common and correctable. Andre notices that he is starting to have trouble on the job. "Holy cow. How did that happen? I have been late for work three times this week." "Let me assess where I am at and take action."

As the counselor gets to know you, they will assess your stage of change, calibrating their techniques to your immediate needs. Considering only the first paragraph of the case study, Andre seems to be in the contemplative stage, recognizing a desire to change but not quite ready to take the steps needed. He is quite ambivalent, and if he tries to work at this early stage, he will likely fail. The MI counselor helps a person resolve ambivalence *before* moving toward a desired goal.

**MI Techniques**

Like CBT, it's nice to work with a therapist when using MI, especially if you are having a really hard time making up your mind about something important. Getting a job is one thing, but quitting drinking or smoking, making a major lifestyle change, and changing your behavior toward other people are not only appropriate for MI, they may necessitate that you get some help with such big changes. When you meet with an MI practitioner, they will probably treat you in two phases. In the initial phase, they will help you resolve your ambivalence and build motivation. In the second phase, they will help to strengthen your commitment and implement a change plan (Arkowitz & Miller, 2008).

To resolve ambivalence, the counselor will help you weigh the pros and cons of each side of your inner conflict. The therapist might ask: "What are the good things about staying on SSI?" "What are the good things about getting a job?" They will pay attention to not only what you say, but how you say it, looking for "change talk," words that indicate that you are moving toward your goal as well as "sustain talk," words that reinforce the status quo. They might say something like this: "On one hand, you have said that it's been nice to get a check for not working, on the other hand, you indicate that having a good income will be a great change. How are you thinking about this change today?" Gradually, the therapist will shift their focus so that they strengthen change talk and redirect sustain talk (Arkowitz & Burke, 2008), all the while helping to reinforce your goal and plan toward the future.

Who would think ambivalence was such a big deal? It really is. In fact, Zuckoff (2015) notes that the more pressing a change is, the more ambivalent we feel. Change plans fail because people never get to the point where they are committed to the plan. MI practitioners, therefore, use a variety of tools to help people move forward. One of these is values clarification. When you understand what you truly care about and why, it's easier to commit to a plan that is aligned with your values. In addition to helping you clarify your values, a therapist might ask the scaling question: "On a scale of one to 10, one being not at all and 10 being 100 percent, how important is this change to you? How ready are you to make this change? How committed are you to making the change?" They might also use affirmations to point out your strengths—feeling genuinely good about yourself helps you to change (Zuckoff, 2015).

**MI on Your Own**

When I was researching this book, I found a great resource: *Finding Your Way to Change: How the Power of Motivational Interviewing Can Reveal What You Want and Help You Get There* by Allan Zuckoff (2015). This is a terrific book that guides you through the process of MI in a self-help format. I read it twice and worked through it, addressing my own ambivalence about dieting and weight loss, a constant theme in my life. I found it extremely helpful. The book provides an MI option for people who don't necessarily want to work with a therapist or just like to engage with self-help books. Are there people like that?

The good news is that MI is a huge help and that being

stuck doesn't have to last forever. Whether you work with a therapist or on your own, you are more likely to follow through on a plan that you created than depend on the advice of other people, which is a key reason why MI helps people commit to a plan. MI is premised on the idea that people are experts on themselves.

Some people express concern that the stages of change include setbacks or relapses. The fact of the matter is that setbacks are the rule, not the exception in life. The fact that setbacks are built into MI makes it realistic. Rather than conceptualize setbacks as failures, MI practitioners see them as a normal part of the process. Setbacks are an opportunity to assess your stage of change and take appropriate action. Even when you have successfully worked through your ambivalence and are maintaining your new behaviors, you can get derailed. This often happens in one of two situations: When things are really stressful or when you become very relaxed and let your guard down. In either case, you might revert to the old behavior (Zuckoff, 2015). The nice thing about MI is that you just need to get back to your plan—no judgment. You can go from a setback to any stage of change, so you're not starting over. Nonetheless, a setback may be difficult because bad feelings can drive the behaviors a person is trying to change, but you still have all of the skills you have learned, and it's all okay.

## The Skinny On Therapy

In summary, do seek counseling to work through your symptoms. I've tried to demystify the process of therapy by describing CBT and MI. You might encounter a counselor who uses other methods such as psychodynamic or person-centered therapy, both of which can be effective as well (although they don't have as much evidence of efficacy as MI and CBT do).

Over my adult life, I have wrestled with symptoms of mental illness. At various times, I have seen a therapist, and I can say, without a doubt, that "talk therapy" is always helpful.

When looking back, however, I can see that therapy is like peeling another layer off an onion. You are not fully changed by the process; instead, your psyche is fresher and newer, although it keeps the same basic contours. We are never fully rid of our worries, our traumas, or our neuroses—these make us who we are. Instead, therapy helps us see them in a new way, providing opportunities to forgive ourselves and others, approach problems with new eyes, and free ourselves from self-defeating thoughts. I think you'll agree that therapy is worth the price of admission. In addition to lots of great therapists in your community, you have access to self-help tools. Take advantage of these! Your quality of life will be better and your ability to work will improve as well.

Lesson Nine: I covered two helpful approaches that can be used in talk therapy, MI and CBT. My goal was to demystify the therapy process, encourage you to take advantage of this wonderful support strategy, and offer you options if you are not yet ready to work with a therapist.

# LESSON TEN:
# MAY I HELP YOU?
# SEEKING AND
# GETTING THE RIGHT
# PROFESSIONAL HELP

We need our care professionals: our psychiatrist, our therapist, our case manager, our social worker, and our primary care doctor. Although they can sometimes make us feel ambivalent, they are the people who are there to help us move forward. Most professionals know intuitively that real healing is not provided through the latest intervention, technique, or pill. It can only be bestowed by a person. If you ask people in recovery what made the difference that allowed them to join the mainstream of life once again, do they mention medications, hospitalization, or rehabilitation programs as pivotal factors in their recovery? They do not. Instead, they will invariably talk about a doctor encountered along the way who really got it or a long suffering and insightful counselor who gave them both strength and strategies when they needed them.

From my own experience, I know that recovery is both intrapersonal (comes from within) *and* interpersonal (happens between people), and that it is fostered by significant relationships with helping professionals, family members, and friends. In my case it was my partner, my clinical team, and my family and friends, who made the difference. Without my partner, certain friends, and my family, I don't know where I would be right now; I surely would not be writing this book. For me, getting better has been a collaborative process, and I have depended on both formal and informal help to move me along my own personal path toward recovery. However, relationships, formal and informal, can be the most elusive and fragile of resources for people with psychiatric disabilities. Relationships often break under the strain of uncontrolled psychiatric symptoms and must be repaired—a task of recovery. In Lesson 10, I specifically address our relationships with professionals. I talk about informal supports in Lesson 11 titled "Support, not just fancy lingerie."

In this lesson, I provide a journal entry and include my analysis to explore the issue of formal supports in their various forms. Good supports go beyond services rendered and include a sense of connection and unconditional regard. Indirectly, I address the professionals who can be relied on for their wise counsel in the face of a crisis. I attempt all of this by providing two examples of professional help; one bad and one good. I leave it to you to sort out which professionals are helpful and harmful in your own life. I end this lesson with a discussion of shared decision-making, a process leading to more productive discussions with psychiatrists and other helping professionals. The moral to the story is that we can choose to be supported well and treated well by others. As our own self-advocates, we call the shots.

## Professional Help

I deeply appreciate the help professionals can provide, and I have cherished my good doctors and therapists over the years. I have written about the invaluable help of professionals in previous chapters. However, professionals have a tremendous responsibility to us. In spite of this fact, professionals can be a detriment when they approach us with unhelpful attitudes. You see, those of us who have a psychiatric diagnosis suffer acutely and painfully from a discredited identity, even by our medical and clinical staff members. We are often seen as "un-persons," as autistic videographer and advocate Mel Baggs puts it. Baggs has a number of videos available on YouTube. I think you'll find them interesting. Using synthesized speech, for she is largely nonverbal, Baggs eloquently warns of the dangers people face when they are seen as un-persons. Being perceived as an un-person means that before I open my mouth to speak, the nurse, the doctor, even the receptionist, believe they know all they need to know about me: I am *a bipolar*. He is *a schizophrenic*. She is *a borderline*.

You don't need to be a person with a psychiatric disability to know what it feels like to be discredited; an un-person. There is always a shock to the system the moment you realize that you have been judged and dismissed, an experience that is common for every human being, but doubly common for us. For example, it is often a dark epiphany when a young woman realizes that she has been embraced or shunned exclusively based on her body shape or facial structure. Young men who lack the requisite athleticism or coolness required to be "one of the gang" have experienced being an un-person. If you can't remember such a moment, hearken back to the first time you had to go to the unemployment office to put in a claim. Consider how your bruised and tender psyche felt when you ran headlong into the brick wall of an uncaring bureaucracy. Think about how your clients or loved ones are often treated when they seek services or apply for benefits. Consider the way pedestrians look through the homeless, mentally ill person as if they were made of thin air; an un-person.

What does it mean to be a good helping professional? Of course, the basic requirement is a solid educational and experiential background. After that, a requisite level of insight and skill is needed to make communication fruitful. But for me, what really separates the men from the boys and the women from the girls is a willingness to sit with me, face-to-face, without judgment or advice, in my hour of deepest pain. This capacity is rarer than one would think. Instead, some people—even helping professionals of all stripes—tend to spout platitudes, tell you what to do, attempt to solve your problem, or try to get you out of their office (or off the phone) to allay their own discomfort and anxiety.

It must take a lot of skill to sit and just hold a person's hand (literally or figuratively) or listen attentively, because it is not all that common. The essay below is a very mild example of what it feels like to be objectified and discredited by a helping professional, how it subtly eats away at self-esteem. The experience of mental illness is not so rarified or unique that it can't be imagined. Most wounds are inflicted by people, and they can be soothed by people, too. The following journal entry illustrates what happens when a person is treated as their label; as a client, as an un-person. In this scenario, I am seeking the help of a general practitioner who is probably aware that I have bipolar disorder, as that designation is in my medical chart.

## How To Turn A Person Into A Patient

The young doctor walks into the examining room where I am sitting on a table, fully clothed but still feeling nervous and vulnerable. Unsmiling, he extends his hand, barely grasps mine, and then draws it back too quickly, saying, "Hello, Miss Olney, I'm Doctor *So-and-So*." Feeling slighted, I want to say, "What a coincidence, my name is Doctor *Olney*." Instead, I meekly utter a greeting, and then go for the kill: "I'm always shocked when my doctor is younger than my students." I am not sure about my motivations here, but I think it has to do with leveling the playing field, as I am getting progressively uncomfortable. I expect a self-deprecating laugh and a reassuring comeback like, "I may be young, but I know all the latest stuff." Instead, I experience an unsettled sensation as he moves around the room, expression unchanged, his retort an angry silence.

I am sitting on the examining table, reluctantly interacting with this man-child, because I need a physical, EKG, and blood work, and my own doctor is on vacation. I need these things because I am going on a doctor-supervised fast in a few days—supervised by other doctors, not this one, thank goodness. Since beginning a regimen of the antidepressant Lexapro followed by Cymbalta a couple years ago, I had gained 50 pounds, and was now considered obese. It happened so quickly that I had not even had time to adjust my body image. I certainly had tried to address the growing problem in less draconian ways, by going to a nutritionist for six months, going to Weight Watchers for six months, and dieting in other, more random ways in between. Each time, I began the change process totally resolved and ready to succeed. Each time I lost a little and then just stayed there. Soon, I got discouraged, and delicious things began worming their way back into my diet: chocolate (just one square, of course), cheese (one little piece won't hurt), and my very favorite food, seconds. Each time I swiftly gained my weight back plus a few pounds.

As this young doc does a cursory examination of my abdomen, I attempt another human exchange. "I have been blessed with good genes." I say, "Even with this weight gain, I am in great health: Low cholesterol, low blood pressure, no diabetes." The guy answers in a monotone, without making eye contact, "You are still at risk." He leaves, saying someone will be in with the EKG equipment. I have a sneaking suspicion that "someone" may not be showing up for a while, so I hop off the table and settle into the chair by the window with a magazine.

As I sit there, I fume a little bit about how I am being treated. I feel dismissed and silenced, and this young man and I are not even equally matched. I am an established scholar; he is new to his craft. I am well into my fifties; he may have just seen his thirtieth birthday. Why is Dr. *So-and-So* treating me in this manner? Of course, my paranoia is always active, even when I am well, so I conclude that he looked at my list of medications and figured I was nuts. As a person with a psychiatric disability, I would be dismissed—an unperson. I thought, "Hey, maybe it's because I am a fat woman (or in more politically correct parlance, a *woman with fatness*)." Fat people are often scorned and discredited, and although this experience is very new to me, I think I have been dismissed by some people because I am now overweight. Or maybe it's because I am a *woman*—fat or thin, it doesn't matter. Or maybe it's our age difference, although I am guessing that his mom and I are exactly the same age, and I would hope that he treats his mother with more regard than he has treated me.

Ten minutes elapse, and then 20. I am reading a good article, a different one now, so I am only a little irritated about the wait. Finally, a young woman pops into the room as says, "Oh! Didn't the doctor tell you to change?" "Uh, no." She smiles, says something noncommittal, hands me a pink paper gown and asks me to put it on. I ask, "Opening in the front or the back?" She answers, "The front, please." The young woman whisks out of the room, promising to return in a minute.

I am back on the examining table. The young woman, a nurse, I presume, preps areas on my ankles, glues on little "terminals" and snaps the wires into place. At one point she explains, "I have to move your breast" and affixes a node on the left side of my ribcage. I jokingly say, "The only good thing about gaining a lot of weight is the awesome boobs." She laughs and later compliments my shoes. I guess this is the easy camaraderie between women, even across generations. I am comforted and balanced by her presence and feel centered again by our very mundane, very human interaction.

After the nurse leaves, I change and sit down to read once again, predicting that it will be a wait. At one point, my eyes wander around the room, and I see some information about the young doctor who is examining me on a bulletin board. Doctor *So-and-So* is interested in prevention, weight loss, diabetes…oh Lordy! This is the kind of thing he wants to be doing! Why doesn't he choose a specialty that will allow him to interact with *unconscious* people all day long? He could be a surgeon. Or better yet, a medical examiner.

As we all know, prevention is about diet, exercise, smoking cessation, stress management—behavior change. To get people to change their familiar, comfortable (but often harmful) behaviors, the health professional needs to encourage, motivate, cheer, empathize—but never judge. If the helping person is on his high horse, he has already galloped miles from where the real help is needed.

I resume reading, as the required 20 minutes of waiting draws to a close, and, as I have not quite finished reading my new article, I slip the magazine into my folder. In 54 years, I have never stolen a magazine from a doctor's office, but there is something about being treated as an un-person that makes me feel slightly hostile. It's my own quiet little protest.

## What Does Good Professional Care Look Like?

We have explored the experience of being treated like an un-person and I'm guessing that many readers have had bad experiences such as the one I convey pretty routinely. Knowing that health care can be invalidating, triggering, and just plain unhelpful, what can you do to be sure that your interactions with professionals are beneficial?

Along the same line, a skilled and sensitive therapist is essential. I am not seeing anyone at the moment, but I can give you a general idea of the kind of support I have found useful. Any doctor or therapist can be good at their craft, but not ideal for you at a given moment in time. For example, insight-oriented therapy (like Freudian counseling) seemed good for me when I was younger. I needed to figure out how my history contributed to and impacted my illness. After a while, I had learned all that I could and continuing in this vein would have only fixated me on the past. During serious crises, I was fortunate to find therapists who could firmly guide me back to full functioning. One such therapist acted as my case manager, locating the resources I needed--a psychiatrist, a neuropsychologist, and a neurologist--when I was too confused to do so for myself. Other therapists were action oriented: They taught me new ways of thinking and reacting, giving me new tools for interacting with the world. My most recent counselor, a cognitive behavioral therapist, provided me with lots of tools for living.

Our general practitioners are also an important part of the team. Insurance companies try to tell you differently, but physical health care is mental health care and vice versa. We are not able to compartmentalize our mental illness to an area above the neck and neither should your doctors. Although my chart announces loudly that I have bipolar disorder, my regular doctor always talks to me as an equal, problem-solving and thinking things through with me. Is it too much to ask high regard from those whose bills we pay? I must admit, though, having my psychiatric label displayed to the world like a scarlet letter gives me pause. I never feel more stigmatized than I do when I go to my general practitioner, not because I feel she judges me, but because the nurses and receptionists have access to that damned label.

As I thought about who would be a good example of professional help, I couldn't help but select my psychiatrist, Dr. H. Since 2006, he has been a central part of what I think of as my team. He literally rescued me from a long, deep depression and continues to help me through the twists and turns of a serious mood disorder. He is compassionate and very respectful. I never feel that he is trying to manipulate me or treat me as inferior to him. I think my psychiatrist sees me as a challenge, and he is both creative and tireless in helping me with my intractable symptoms. These are, of course, qualities you'd expect in all psychiatrists--but you would be mistaken. Dr. H. always greets me as an equal, stays calm in a crisis, and celebrates my successes. It's almost as if he was born to do this work. When I leave his office, I feel as though I was fully heard and that my views figured into *our* medical decisions. My questions about medications are met with facts and rational arguments. For example, I have worried about the impact of lithium on my organs and asked Dr. H. about reducing or discontinuing the medication. He explained (to my satisfaction) that lithium was controlling my manic symptoms and that he monitors my bloodwork to assure that my kidneys are not negatively impacted by the drug. He allayed my concerns with facts: because he is monitoring me, lithium is a safe drug for me. We discussed the science. I left this meeting feeling confident in him and in my medications, glad that I can discuss my concerns. Dr. H. will listen carefully, taking my concerns into account, but providing the scientific explanations that I need to be secure in my decisions.

Psychopharmacology is the profession of prescribing and monitoring psychiatric medications. Each meeting is 15-minutes long, and the doctor must ask the right questions and use their best guessing abilities to come up with a medication or medications that are going to be helpful to you. I talk to a lot of people who still have uncontrolled symptoms or unpleasant side effects from their medications and I wonder why they don't continue their search for a more appropriate medication. Dr. H. always promised that I would be symptom and side-effect free and, after trying perhaps a dozen medications over 15 years, I am. A really good psychopharmacologist will keep working with you until you find that sweet spot: controlled symptoms without undue physical or mental distress.

The moral to the story is that you never have to be treated badly by professionals. As you evaluate your professional helpers, think about the way they make you feel, both when you're in their office and on their medication. Consider what kinds of conversations you have had with them. Do they listen to you? Collaborate with you? The following section is about shared decision-making, a process that can help you better work with your doctor or helping professional. Dr. H. does it naturally and I would guess that any intelligent helping professional can learn how to share with you.

## What Is Shared Decision-Making?

Learning to manage a psychiatric disability, including learning how to take medications, is not an all or nothing proposition. According to Deegan (2007), taking medications is an "active, self-determining stance," not one of compliance (p. 63). The underlying assumption of shared decision-making is that, when consulting with an expert, there are actually two experts in the room. The doctor is an expert on the various medications, their actions, purposes, side-effects, and courses. People with psychiatric disabilities are experts on their own lives, their bodies, their reactions to medication, their symptoms, and what is effective. The two experts respectfully work together to manage the psychiatric symptoms, medications, and medication side effects (Deegan & Drake, 2006). By collaborating with psychiatrists and other clinicians, we take active control of our recovery. Professionals reap the benefit of working with people who are participants in their own recovery and engaged in figuring out how to let the professionals help them. Patients benefit from working with a doctor who listens to them and takes their experiences and perspectives into account when considering various medications. Through collaboration and hard work, people with psychiatric disabilities become experts in our own journey of recovery (Deegan, 1996).

Many people stay tied to helping professionals who are not truly helping. As you make your list of the helping professionals in your life, consider each person carefully. Do you feel confident that you can reach out to this professional in a crisis? Are you able to discuss the pros and cons of various treatment options, or does the professional dictate to you what you should do?

Lesson 10: Getting the Right Help covered cultivating a

team of caring and skilled professionals who share decision-making with you, and who will be there for you. Honestly, this is better than any insurance policy. But like insurance, relationships with professionals have a cost—your money, your valuable time, and your trust.

# LESSON ELEVEN: SUPPORT: NOT JUST FANCY LINGERIE

In Lesson 10, I talked about professional help. Here I address the other side of the equation: informal supports. Over the course of the book, we have explored a wide array of supports and strategies including medications, job accommodations, career resources, and therapy. However, without the informal supports that we get from our family members and friends, getting well and staying well would be a monumental challenge. It deserves its own lesson.

My friend Jemma wrote about a time when she was there to help me in a crisis. A decade ago I called her and asked her to sit with me when I was having auditory hallucinations. Jemma sat with me for most of a day. In the essay that follows, Jemma provides insights into not only my behavior but hers as well. She gives sage advice for clinicians, family members, and friends who want to help but are unsure of what to do or how to do it. As an insightful, experienced professional, Jemma knows how to behave in a crisis. Below, she describes our day together, explaining how to simply be with someone who is experiencing difficulties.

## Being Present: Jemma's Perspective (Essay By A Friend)

### The Phone Call

"Hold on a minute Lynda, someone is calling on my cell."

"Hello, good afternoon!"

"Good afternoon Jemma, could you come over? I am having auditory hallucinations. I was going to take my shower and I am hearing very loud screaming and it is a little scary."

"I'll be right there."

"Lynda, I have to go."

## The Importance of Having Someone to Call/Having a Good Support System

It is very important for people with mental illnesses to have someone they can call when they are experiencing difficult times. Having a good support system in place, which consists of people with whom they can feel safe and comfortable, is an important aspect of the recovery/healing process for individuals with psychiatric disorders. It has been my experience that in order to be effective and to contribute positively to the healing process of our loved ones in their time of crisis is to remain cognizant of the fact that at that specific time, the moment, or the hour, or whatever length of time our presence may be needed, it is all about that individual. We are not there to make things right, or to teach, or to provide anything but loving support to help the individual feel safe and able to cope with whatever they perceive to be their problem at that precise time. The best way I find this can be done is just by being totally present, mind, body, and soul, with a heart full of genuine love. This can be accomplished by attentive and empathic listening with an open mind and with the willingness to learn, not trying to formulate answers or magic potions while they are trying to explain to us what they are experiencing. Remember our loved ones or clients are inviting us into their world, therefore it is imperative that we remain respectful and receptive and meet our loved ones where they are at that given time.

## Upon Arrival

I arrived at my friend's house approximately thirty minutes after receiving her phone call. After greeting me at the door my friend started to explain her current experience with auditory hallucinations, which she described as being "different this time. I have had auditory hallucinations in the past but not like this. This time there was a lot of loud screaming and that scared me a little."

We walked from the living room into the kitchen and my eyes followed the scan of my friend's hand and I beheld small neat piles of books, stacks of papers, and pictures throughout the house. I was thinking to myself, this is a familiar sign of mania. My thoughts were interrupted by the sound my friend's voice saying, "I have many projects going as you can tell, you can help me if you want to or you can just sit and read, whatever you want to do is fine with me; I am just happy that you are here."

**Being Present**

If we listen carefully we will realize that our loved ones tell us exactly what they need or want from us. It was not important to my friend that I help her with her projects, I could just sit there and read; she said it all in her statement "I am just happy that you are here." She did not need me to "fix" her or her situation. She just wanted to feel safe.

As family members or friends, it would benefit us to respect our loved one's outreach to us as invitations for them to help us understand their perceptions of the voices or images that torment their lives or whatever discomfort they may be experiencing currently. We will then be able to listen to their plight with an attitude of respect and a willingness to learn, and a desire to understand. This manner of listening will lead us to ask questions such as: How may I help or be of service to you? Rather than approaching them with our preconceived notions, and rushing into clinical evaluations and diagnosis, a laundry list of labels, and being ready to solve their problem.

By listening with a respectful attitude, and by asking the individual to tell us how we may help or be of service to them, we will be accomplishing the following:

- We will be showing respect and validating the

individual's beliefs, and their perception of their mental illness.

- We will also be earning the individual's respect while gaining their trust.
- We will be building better rapport with them
- We will also be empowering the person and helping them to recognize that they have an active role in their recovery.

I believe that this method of approach will allow service providers to successfully implement their evidenced-based practices (EBP) such as motivational interviewing (MI), and cognitive behavior therapy (CBT) at the appropriate time, which is when the individual is ready to be receptive and is willing to work on action steps which they participated in developing.

**Listening and Observing**

I followed my friend around in her kitchen then back into the living room as she pointed out her uncompleted projects. I decided to sit in the living room and browse through one of her many Frida Kahlo books. My friend continued walking around in the kitchen area. After a few minutes, she came into the living room, laid down on the couch and proceeded to describe her auditory hallucinations and her emotions surrounding this experience. I carefully replaced the book on the bookshelf and gave my undivided attention to my friend, because I was curious and very interested not only in what she was saying but also in her expression and actions as she spoke.

Her body language was playful and almost childlike for a moment as she lay on the couch knees bent and smoothing her hair away from her face. This lasted only a few minutes before she was up again, this time with a business-like expression stating she had to make two phone calls. Back to the kitchen she whisked and proceeded to make her phone calls, pacing the kitchen floor as she conversed with her contacts. After ending her phone calls my friend returned to the living room and inquired whether or not I was interested in going shopping for a while because she "had some errands to run." I was only too happy to oblige because being with my friend is a sheer delight and as strange as it may sound I enjoy being with her when she is manic. Together we organized her piles and put them away and off we went. "TUESDAY MORNING."

This interaction, from my friend Jemma's point of view, provides guidance on how a friend or family member can just be there for you, without judgment, without trying to fix it. Jemma is the ideal friend in this regard. As a trained counselor, she knows when it is and isn't appropriate to counsel or give advice. In this instance, I used my WRAP to reach out to a friend in a crisis, and she was able to be there with me and for me. Jemma listened and followed my lead; she never counseled me or told me what to do. She even went bargain shopping with her manic friend (Tuesday Morning is really cool a bargain store). Any good friend or family member can provide this kind of support, and it's important for you to have people you can call on in a crisis, who will just sit with you. I have been fortunate to have relationships with other friends who will literally sit with me, and that's often enough.

I do lots of things each day to maintain my wellness such as relaxing with a good book or television, eating three nutritious meals each day, and checking at least a few items off my to-do list. I make sure to include regular workouts and walks, medication check-ups, hot baths, shopping, and haircuts. But what is most important? It is the support system in my life: my daily private time with Sharon, weekly calls with my sister, and regular visits with my friends and family. I know what to do if I'm experiencing symptoms—things I have learned through trial and error over the years and through the process of developing my own WRAP—such as clearing my calendar and taking a mental health day when I wake up feeling depressed, or slowing down and getting a good night's sleep when I'm feeling manic. Calling a close friend to come sit with me when symptoms are scary means tapping into that network of support. It's just good to know I'm safe and cared for, no matter what.

One of the hardest things to deal with for people with psychiatric disabilities is that their potential networks of support are damaged due to past crises, or dusty from disuse. A critical skill for any person in recovery is to build that network back up. Sometimes a therapist can be helpful in assisting you as you brainstorm ways to get people back into your life. Joining a support group or taking a class (maybe a WRAP class in your community) can provide the opportunity to begin the rebuilding process. Sometimes there will need to be difficult conversations with parents or siblings who you have either neglected or misused in the past. Believe me, these hard conversations are worth it, because if you take every bit of my advice and you are still lacking support, your recovery is fragile at best.

## Family Support

I've highlighted what a friend can do for you in a crisis situation. What about everyday life? How do I meet my need for human connection, the kind of caring relationships that can lead to healing? Although she probably didn't know it at the time, my mother was and is an important figure in my recovery. The following journal entry, written years ago, illustrates—through the metaphor of my garden—who she is to me and her helping role in my life.

## My Garden Reclaimed (Journal Entry)

I can't talk about the wonderful changes in my garden without giving tribute to my mother. You see, my mother came and stayed with us again this Christmas. She was the one who made sure the tasks I had saved up for my winter break got ticked off the list, one-by-one. If I had been left to my own devices, I would have read book after book. There are no *tasks deferred* with my mother around.

Describing something as complex, colorful, and alive as a garden stretches my skills as a writer, but I know I can provide the then-and-now contrasts that will give you the visual images you need to fully appreciate the transformation of my back patio. Imagine a flagstone courtyard surrounded by a wall with a border of weedy soil all the way around it. An occasional plant, yellowed, toughened, dusty, peaks out of the dry, lumpy dirt. Yes, there is green in addition to grey and yellow—every square inch of the available soil is covered in green weeds. The sight of this is so sad that I have spent several years just running through the courtyard to get to the garage, never stopping to have a glass of wine in the warm California sun, seated at the table placed invitingly in the center of the space. This place that should be Eden is a wasteland.

The ruined garden has been a living, growing metaphor —a constant reminder of the distraction, the debilitation that is psychiatric disability. When I was better, I spent every available moment in the garden, tending, nurturing, scheming vistas of beauty, and then letting nature do the work of creating a masterpiece. I surrounded myself and my loved ones with colors, textures, and blossoms more subtle, complex, and searingly beautiful than anything a great artist could put on canvas. For years, I had the habit of visiting my garden each morning. Examining each and every plant: "Does this one need water? Is that some sign of disease? Is this area getting a little crowded? Oops, there's a little weed." This fifteen-minute ritual is almost guaranteed to keep everyone in the garden happy and gorgeous. I was passionate about gardening and spent every possible minute doing it. It was my meditation, my creative outlet.

It was tragic for me when I lost gardening. It started when I moved from the Northeast side of the country to the Midwest, and then to the Southwest. Moving always results in the loss of friends, and this applies to plants as well as people. Whereas I had for years surrounded myself with Iris, Astilbe, Peony,

Tulip, Coneflower, and even Forget-Me-Not (who I have never forgotten), I now had California plants that were equally pretty, but had unfamiliar names, habits, and needs. I was sad without my friends, both human and horticultural. I felt kind of lost.

Sadness became depression with the familiar anhedonia, the inability to feel pleasure. These periods were, occasionally, relieved by periods of high mood, high productivity and poor judgment. The flurries of activity were goal-driven, but the task lists rarely included reclaiming the garden. For two years now, I have been feeling progressively better, more balanced. I revel in the knowledge that it's coming back—I am coming back.

Enter my mother: a gentle, unassuming yet funny, smart, and tough-as-nails woman. Although she doesn't like to think there is mental illness in our family, she is sorely mistaken on this one point. Otherwise, she is sensible, healthy, and centered.

It makes me laugh that my mom still gives me a hard time about being spoiled. During our extended visit, she gently teased me about this again. I kiddingly responded "And whose fault it that?" Mom again told the story about her being diagnosed with breast cancer when I was only 18 months old. She was very young with four little kids at home. It was 1956 and treatments for breast cancer were nearly nonexistent. Premenopausal breast cancer has a much worse prognosis than breast cancer in older women, so things did not look good. A surgeon lopped off her breast and sent her back home. Mom says she worried about me growing up without a mother, a rational fear, and as a consequence, pampered me too much and too long. When she tells this story, I feel glad that I could be her "baby" when she needed me. Perhaps I was like a human garden that she could focus on, tend, and nurture to avoid the very real terror of dying at 34. Mom and I have a special bond to this day. My mother is a beautiful person, inside and out, and I feel privileged to have her close to me. I'm always eager to see her and spend time with her even though there are 3000 miles between us.

Looking through the bedroom window and seeing one's

elderly mother in one's own ruined garden, energetically digging, cutting and hauling, would inspire a cadaver into action. Of course, I joined her at once. I learned a few things right away: Gardening is physically demanding, and for a woman who is both over fifty years old and fifty pounds overweight, it is enough to make one want to cry. Getting up and down off the ground hurt my knees and bending over made it hard to breathe. I clearly remember how I used to pop up and down, lean and bend, pull and push, a thousand times an hour. Now, each movement was a momentous event. All the while, my mother was vigorously, nimbly, dancing through my garden. Inspiration!

You should see the garden now. We have planted canna lilies, some tall, some shorter, bromeliads, agapanthus, lavender, all kinds of succulents and cacti. These are some of the unfamiliar tropical and California plants that I could not warm up to initially. The dried up, pitiful hydrangea has been moved from a place in the sun that it hated to a big pot in the shade. The palms have been fed their special food and the camellia has had hers as well. We have window boxes ready for the lovely purple African daisies that have taken over the shade garden. (Sharon wants them out of there so that they won't compete with the fig tree. I am certain that it does no harm to underplant a tree, but I will perform a rare act of compliance and simply make it so without argument.)

The garden is largely potential right now, but looking very tidy and bursting with hope. The canna blossoms will soon emerge and make a stunning display of red and gold all along the wall. The flowering plants will flower in their unique and utterly amazing way. The palms will gradually metamorphose from sickly yellow to deep, dusty green. It's all good. And, again, I'm glad to share in the magical metamorphosis by doing a little blooming myself. If I learned anything from my mother today it was that relationships need tending, just as plants do. Thank you, Mom.

In addition to Sharon and my mother, my sister Karen has been a constant source of support and sanity. Also labeled with bipolar disorder, she has struggled mightily and has the insight and patience to help keep me on an even keel. My sisters Judith and Gini, my brother Tom, and my nieces and nephews have also been in occasional contact, reminding me daily that I am a member of a circle of mutual support. There are friends, and I have had wonderful friends, but as exciting as these relationships can be, I have never leaned on them the way I have my family. Your family is kind of stuck with you, and that can be a good thing.

I have had such dear friends (plant and human), first in upstate New York where we had a network of people, endless dinner parties, and good intentions to become champion meditators (which were mostly aspirational). Living in the Midwest for five years, I made instant and lasting friendships at my university, people I love and stay close to, sometimes every few months, other times, over the years. We had a circle of friends there as well, and we miss the parties, the conversations, the closeness. California has been more of a challenge. Although I share warmth and closeness with certain colleagues, populating our lives with other people we enjoy and who like us has not come easy, with a few key exceptions. Looking over the landscape of my life and seeing such a dearth of friends can be discouraging. I realize that in order to nurture real friendships, I'll need to take some risks, get my trowel in there and start digging.

One of the most important things about managing a mental illness is having good, human support. Professionals play a role in this, but, as I've demonstrated, having friends and family members close is paramount. And we must repair and maintain those relationships, much like you would a garden. The labor that goes into making that phone call to your brother or having that lunch with a friend pays off in ways you can only imagine.

Mary Ellen Copeland, author of the WRAP that I introduced in Lesson 2, suggests that you have a list of five people you can call on if you need help. These can be therapists, family members, friends, even your supervisor, but they need to be people who know you and care about you. Five is a number to aspire to, knowing that it's people that keep us well. If relationships need repair, consider how you might fix them. If you don't have enough people in your life, consider how you might find more. In my own research, several people found a circle of friends by taking a WRAP class in their community. One group of women checks on each other every day (Olney & Emery-Flores, 2017).

Lesson Eleven: Support takes many forms and is essential to your recovery. Having a circle of support, mutual relationships, is an important insurance policy. More than that, though, mutual friendships sustain us through good times and bad.

# LESSON TWELVE:
# KNOW YOURSELF:
# YOUR GATEWAY
# TO INSIGHT

Insight is a critical ingredient of recovery, and there are many ways to increase your self-awareness. A primary tool for me has been writing. I find that the writing process helps me delve in deeply and come away with new insights about myself and my world. In fact, I never profoundly understand what I think or feel until I write about it. You may find this to be true as well. Another obvious gateway to insight is reading —about psychiatric rehabilitation and mental health, yes, but also about a wide range of topics. Knowledge naturally leads to self-understanding, and knowing yourself gives you insight into what makes you tick. Having insight provides you with the resources you need to maintain your stability and get through crises.

So, there is reading and writing...what else? Therapy is designed to help you not only work the kinks out of your psyche, but to gain deep insights into yourself. Talking to friends and family members can also stimulate personal growth. Discussing and sharing with others, professionals or loved ones, provides a great opportunity for developing insight into yourself while building relationships. Support groups sponsored by the National Association for Mental Illness (NAMI) or the Depression and Bipolar Support Association (DBSA), a WRAP group, or even a book club provides ways to develop as a person and simultaneously create closer connections with others. By going out and joining a group, you may even find new people to add to your list of supporters.

I have found that meditation and yoga give my brain the break it needs to step back and examine itself. A little mental quietness creates a space for new connections to fall into place. Whether you quiet your mind through meditation, yoga, or prayer, you'll find that a quiet mind is a receptive mind. Another thing that can quiet my mind is being in nature. I love the beach, the cliffs, and the woods, but your place may be in the mountains, a lake, or staring at a big, blue sky. I find that getting outside and finding some beauty there gets my mind off the dailiness of life and on to the bigger issues. You may have a favorite place that you return to over and over or find that you are ready to explore new vistas. Let nature transport you and give you joy.

Engaging in the arts, or appreciating the arts can also take your mind to a new place, whether you are finger painting or visiting a museum, listening to music or singing in a choir, you'll find yourself transported, leaving an opening for new self-understanding. There are as many strategies for increasing insight as there are thinkers in the world. I'm sure I missed some but hope these few ideas spark your interest.

## Why Should I Work Toward Deeper Self-Understanding?

Don't be afraid to delve into your innermost thoughts and fears. To put your mind at ease, I am going to share a secret with you: we all know madness on some level. If you peruse the *Diagnostic and Statistical Manual of Mental Disorders* (DSM-5), you will spot traits on every page that echo your own quirks or those of your loved ones. When I shared some of my journal entries with my three sisters, two of them said, "I feel like that all the time!" The third is also diagnosed with bipolar disorder, so I knew she could relate, but the responses of my "well" sisters surprised me. From these exchanges, I gained the following insight about myself and my symptoms: I am not any crazier than anyone else. Even severe symptoms make sense if they are considered in context. The progression from emotionally overwrought, to unbalanced, to suspicious, to paranoid, to delusional, to psychotic is simply that: a continuum. It's the severity of the symptoms, the frequency, and most critically, the impact of these episodes on my ability to stay employed and maintain relationships, that ultimately distinguish problems of daily living from incapacitation. Sigmund Freud may not have a lot of relevance in modern times, but it was he who said work and love are the tasks of adulthood, and I fully agree with him (on this one point, mind you).

Based on years of experience, I understand psychiatric disability as a provider of services, as a consumer of services, as a scholar who studies psychiatric rehabilitation, and as a person who lives and breathes the tools of recovery, so you can trust me to steer you in the right direction when it comes to the importance to your recovery of developing deeper insights into yourself. In this lesson, my intention is to provide you with a model of insight-oriented self-exploration. I start by creating my own timeline, continue by analyzing my symptoms and how I deal with them, and end with a reflection on my fears. As you will see, I am doing dangerous work here, making myself vulnerable, but I'm hoping that by doing so, that you will have some models of self-exploration and you will develop greater insight-oriented skills.

Dr. Monica Ramirez Basco (2006), a CBT expert and author of *The Bipolar Workbook* and several other excellent publications about bipolar disorder, suggests that you create a timeline to get a handle on your history of mental illness. I do that here, touching on my childhood and exploring how I got from there to where I am now, or at least how ages four through eighteen featured in my development. I found the process of writing about this material not only helped me understand who I was as a child, it also gave me important insights into the forces that made me who I am. By providing you with this example from my own life, I am encouraging you to create your own timeline.

## Creating A Timeline (Writing Activity)

My first real memory of being alive was lying in bed pondering my existence. "I am me" kept going through my head, as I thought about my separateness, the parameters of my body, the scary and delightful feeling of being alone and apart. I could not have been older than three or four. As I grew up, I always felt different. I had friends, played, and tried to fulfill my roles as daughter, sister, partner, friend, student, and employee but always saw myself as outside and apart. I was considered odd. In my freshman year I was approached by sororities and boys, who quickly figured out that I was something of a weirdo and hastily changed their minds. This was fine by me! Happily, I reached adolescence during the twilight of the hippy era, and the nonconformist, mind-expanding philosophy of the day was a terrific smoke screen for me.

People are incredulous when I tell them that I was a horrible student when I was young. Considering my choice of career as a university professor, it seems impossible now that I barely made it through high school. I believe I was largely self-educated. I spent my high school years sitting in the back of class, reading all the existentialists from the tiny books I kept hidden behind my big text when I should have been learning geometry. I drew and I wrote during class. As early as seventh grade, I was sent to the school guidance counselor because the drawings in the margins of paper I submitted were, shall we say, unusual. The teacher was convinced that I was on drugs— I was not. Even in 1968, few 12-year-olds in the suburbs were experimenting with drugs.

Later, my friend Jimmy and I broke into the guidance

counselor's office and took a look at our files. Okay, we really didn't break in as much as walk in when the counselor was elsewhere. In those files I found my first label: "high potential, low achiever." I also found my IQ score, a sacred number that is, for some unknown reason, strongly guarded against discovery (although not guarded well enough from rascals like Jimmy and me). I never had any individualized help or counseling to remedy the low-achiever label and apparently my potential remained intact in spite of the benign neglect of my school. I continued to do poorly in courses I didn't like and excel in the ones I did like. Typically, I relied on my exam grades to get me through school. I seem to have a facility with standardized tests in spite of deficient general knowledge of some topics, like math and science. I won a full scholarship to any state university in New York State by taking the Regents Scholarship Exam. I was the college-bound kid graduating near the bottom of her class. Yay, tests!

This was not by design. I realize that it sounds like bragging to say one never had to work to succeed. First, I wanted desperately to do what was expected of me. I was in torment over my parents' anger and disappointment. I simply did not know how to do what was required. Second, I have reached the limits of my intellectual abilities on more than one occasion now, and see my gifts as modest. I guess that high school isn't very challenging for a young girl who is very well-read.

The end of adolescence is where I will leave my timeline as I have told you about my early career and my adult life throughout the book. You should be able to piece together your history given some peace and quiet and a pen and paper.

Let's unpack this. When it comes to my timeline, questions of difference and conformity come to the fore. It is human to want to be accepted, to be part of the group. It is equally human to want to stand out from the crowd. Thus, my dilemma with sacrificing individuality for acceptance is fairly standard. However, my experience of differentness was and still is a very painful one when the nonconforming behavior is unintentional, assessed negatively, and used as a wedge to cut me off from others. The recovery question remains: How much should an individual be expected to conform to others' expectations in order to be accepted into the group? After 50 years, I am still puzzled by this. What has your life been like? Who influenced you? What puzzles you about yourself, your history, and your behavior?

## Three Symptoms, A Thousand Strategies

I find that, due to my disability, I still cannot truly understand the experience that people call "normal." At one point, my self-awareness task was to find out about "normal" and see if I could figure out what that feels like. I have long known that normal feelings are not only typical feelings, they are there to give us critical information about the world around us and our own behavior. When we do something crappy, we feel guilty; when we do something good for someone else it makes us feel good. However, in my experience with a mood disorder, feelings go off on their own without regard for me, other people, events, or even the situation. This is true for mania. It is equally true for depression and doubly true for paranoia. Here I try my hand at describing depression, mania, and paranoia knowing that someone else's experience with symptoms might be very different from mine, but hoping that readers accept my invitation to examine their own symptoms in light of their history, current circumstances, and plans for the future.

### What is Depression Like?

In trying to describe depression, I have said, "It feels like my best friend has died." Or "It's the end of the world." The unspoken part is "and it's my fault." The sense of doom, guilt, worthlessness, of being sick to my core with bad feelings can be utterly overwhelming, or can be an intrusive presence lurking just beyond my conscious awareness, only to emerge, genie-like, at any real or imagined slight. It is hearing the voices of others disparage me from the next room. It is not being able to read or think, staring into space or into a television screen for a good bit of the day. It looks placid; immobile from the outside; it feels like a fire storm on the inside.

I recently read William Styron's 1990 account: *Darkness Visible: A Memoir of Madness* in which he describes a depressive episode. The visceral, palpable description of immobility, horror, and utter sickness matched my own experience much better than the symptoms listed in the DSM-5. My depression bears no resemblance to "I'm depressed, my boyfriend left me," or "I'm depressed, I didn't get that promotion I wanted." One of the most difficult things about depression is that other people think they know what that word means; they think it's an experience we share.

Depression, like all psychiatric symptoms is cognitive as well as emotional. You feel differently but you also *think* differently. Depression alters perceptions as significantly as mania does. Most people don't understand this, and they are perplexed, even angry, when a loved one attempts or completes a suicide. Whereas the individual was probably thinking that the world would be a better place without them, the loved one often registers the suicide as a hostile act, perhaps even intended to punish them. The cognitive distortions are on both sides of the conversation: in reality, the world will be a sadder and emptier place without that individual, and the suicidal person was probably not punishing anyone but themselves. Over the years, perhaps since Sigmund Freud (no, I don't quite understand why his name is coming up again), we have attended to emotion and its role in causing and perpetuating mental illness. However, you can't understand mental illness without attending to the emotional *and* the cognitive nature of these disabilities.

How do I know it when I am not depressed? Recently I had a necessary but highly unpleasant confrontation with some of my students. They were terribly upset by it and, because I am a tender and empathetic being, their feelings resonated with me. Over the next two days, I felt slightly guilty and more than a little regretful. I registered those familiar feelings as depressive symptoms, and even wondered if I might be getting sick again. Then it struck me: Aha! These are "normal" feelings. They are the feelings of empathy, guilt, and regret, only in small doses rather than in a deluge. I was feeling the pain and embarrassment of others, and regretting that I had a hand in it. I was *not* getting sick! Instead, my feelings were giving me accurate and helpful feedback, just like nature intended.

## What is Mania Like?

In my quest for insight, I have explored mania many times and in multiple ways. Here is one journal entry, written during my last crisis, that captures my experience with mania.

## Mania Is A Drug (Journal Entry)

I awake, fully energized and brimming with great ideas. My partner gently puts her arm around my waist, barely conscious. I begin talking: about the cat, the noise from the refrigerator, the time. "What time is it?" I open my cell phone. 1:09 AM. Ladies and gentlemen, she's off and running!

In the last two days, it has dawned on me that I might be in a little bit of trouble. Oh, yes, I have noticed that my moods are "expansive" and my energy is high. I'm working even more than usual and starting to lose my ability to focus due to excess energy. Sometimes I find it hard to just sit in a chair. I find it hard to shut up. I feel vaguely hostile and don't much care who knows it. The best indicator that the balance has tipped: people around me are getting upset. My partner is at the point of pulling her hair out. My graduate assistant is devastated by my harsh feedback. The contractors who are remodeling our kitchen all show up within an hour—the wall guy, the plumber, the painter, the guy for the baseboards, and the person who I hope is going to make my cabinets materialize—to ask me if everything is okay. I ask a new friend on the phone why she didn't give me feedback about this behavior, and she replies, "I didn't know whether you would get upset or angry." All objective indictors point to one fact: I'm manic.

As people with bipolar disorder go, I am good at insight, but the only way I can detect this ascent into mania is by looking at the faces and listening to the voices of other people— concerned, angry, hurt, cautious. Inside my skin, I feel right. No, I don't mean well, I mean that inside my subjective reality, I am absolutely correct in my perceptions and beliefs and behaviors. It's when I see the results of these that I start to doubt myself. That's when the familiar, naked sensation of being wrong, being *publicly* wrong, returns. Something is not right.

When my partner says, in exasperation, "You had better take that evening lithium. You're not thinking right," it's time to face the truth and take some corrective action. That action requires soul searching. Let's start with the evening lithium. I have been experiencing high energy and even more than my usual intensity for several weeks and I have not been taking the lithium as prescribed. It started when I came out of a short depression. The depression came on the heels of a trip across country during which I took a red eye to the east coast, stayed a couple of days, and flew back. This *after* spending a week alone, without my partner's moderating influences on my behavior, without her making sure I slept at night. Unfortunately, bipolar disorder is the only illness that makes one feel better the less sleep one gets.

I went along for a month, functioning adequately; at

least that's what I thought. I must have known on some level that something wasn't totally right, because I often thought about that evening lithium. "Should I take it?" "No, wait until tomorrow and see how you feel then." You see, mania tends to distort the truth. In reality, I was climbing higher by the day, and I knew what to do about it. I just couldn't bring myself to do it. "Maybe tomorrow."

Mania is an addiction. Like other addicts, I use self-deception to keep the high. This time, I wasn't even beyond misleading my partner and my psychiatrist, who just assumed I was taking that evening lithium. *Okay, now I am taking it!*

The bigger issue now becomes, "How do I make amends?" I hope I was not flying high long enough to do any lasting damage to my relationships or career. When I spoke with my graduate assistant yesterday, I apologized about the harsh feedback I had given her, thanking her for her consistently excellent results and her tremendous help to me over the years. Making peace with my partner may prove more difficult. I sense that she is fed up to the point of desperation.

I reiterate: manic depression is an addictive, mind-altering drug. Like all addicts, I need to acknowledge that, yes, I am powerless to control it. However, I must do so, for no person or thing has responsibility for my actions except me. It's so easy to say, "It wasn't me, it was the mania," but that doesn't cut it. God, I hate the morning after!

In talking with my therapist, I tried to sort out how to tell if I am getting manic. As I mention in this essay, the experience of mania comes with a subjective sense of utter rightness. This is a false center: With mania comes distorted thinking, and it is hard to fight one's own distortions. I have asked Sharon and other friends to please let me know if my behavior seems out of proportion with a given situation, unwise or extreme. It's harder to get this kind of feedback than one might imagine. This has meant staying on the road to self-destruction much longer than advisable too many times. Why don't people give their honest feedback when asked?

I have several theories. Asking other people to monitor your behavior can put undue pressure on them. People find it easier to give pro-social responses than to tell you what they are really seeing. Alternatively, other people may get vicarious enjoyment from seeing someone else confront stupidity, dishonesty, and callousness. A hypomanic (or mildly manic) colleague can be counted on to say what other people have the good sense to only think, or possibly discuss with their spouse if they are steamed enough. Hypomanic people are entertaining to be with. They have tons of ideas which they express with drama and complete certainty. Other people enjoy your soliloquy as you articulate their fantasy of kicking someone's ass (verbally, of course) who has been begging for it and richly deserves it. The other person may see you as fearless (foolishly true, at least for the moment); as the avenging angel.

The electric-light symptoms of mania are well-known—excesses in work, in relationships, talking, and even shopping—and certainly, for people who love those of us who have bipolar disorder, manic behavior is easy to spot. So, I shook my head with a combination of embarrassment, disbelief, and recognition, acknowledging another impulsive and thoughtless act, and said to my friend, "I wonder what it would be like if I were this way all the time." My friend said, "You'd have lots of shoes and no friends." Knowing these things is unpleasant, but still worthy of exploration—with the goal of gaining greater insight and being more effective in life.

It is critical to gain insight about how you are impacting other people due to symptoms such as depression or mania. It might seem to make sense to ask for this kind of feedback from the five people in your circle, but don't expect a direct answer. For this kind of insight, you might want to seek out a trained and skilled therapist who will delve into your behaviors, motivations, and goals with you. After all, this is exactly what they are paid to do!

**What are Delusions Like?**

Let's start by saying that paranoia is delusional. Delusions are, by definition, symptoms of psychosis, so I'm not very comfortable owning up to the fact that I'm delusional some of the time. For me, paranoia feels for all the world like everyone is talking about me but believe you me when I say they are not. Because I have experienced a great deal of paranoia over the years, I have learned to manage the sick sensation that I get in response to the perception that people are talking behind my back or judging me negatively. For me, paranoia is paired with depression and is an excellent predictor of a shift in mood to the negative pole. It is never welcome, but I know now to fasten-my-seat-belt-and-bring-my-seat-to-the-full-upright-and-locked-position, as it were. In other words, paranoia is the symptom that tells me I am in for a bumpy ride. In the following days, weeks, or months, I expend much of my emotional energy countering negative thoughts while at work, just to get through my daily routines.

When paranoia strikes, I can hear conversations about me all over the building. As I sit in my corner office, I am assaulted with a cacophony of voices, magnified but muddled, all disparaging me. As you can imagine, these are not productive days. I have learned to counter the beliefs, perceptions, and feelings of delusional thinking with more rational thoughts such as "People like me"; "If people are talking about me, they are probably saying nice things"; and my personal favorite, borrowed from my mother, "Why would they talk about me? I'm just not all that interesting."

These are just a few of the issues I grapple with when it comes to delusional thoughts. As always, there is a grain of truth in all of these symptoms. For example, I don't think that I missed out on learning all of the fine points of social interactions but I am sure that I think differently and react differently than other people do. I have a quirky sense of humor and I often feel like I'm out of step with others. Moreover, what I'm seeing in people may not be accurate and I have no way of knowing because even if I ask a colleague, he or she may not tell me the truth. All of these factors serve to make me more paranoid: What if this drama is all in my head? What if there is no resolution to the paranoia and its causes?

**Symptoms Autopsy**

So, that's depression. That's mania. That's paranoia. You can see why developing insight is such an important and difficult task when I can't trust my feelings to be an accurate reflection of my world and relationships. Because of my symptoms, healthy good feelings, those of mine and others', are difficult for me to detect. Examining how you experience symptoms could add to your insight about your psychiatric disability. I know it has helped me.

It is as hard to detect a subtle or gradual shift in demeanor and behavior—on the way up, down, or sideways—for the observer as it is for the person experiencing these changes. They may see something —mistaken beliefs, unusually low self-esteem, greater confidence, more sadness—but they can't be sure. This point is courtesy of my therapist. In all fairness, I would say the therapist's assessment is probably the closest to true.

# Falling As A Metaphor

A big part of developing insight is coming to grips with your fears. During my most recent mental health crisis, I began frequently falling down, resulting in a fear of steps and stairs. It seemed to start when I fell while viewing the monuments in Washington, DC. This big, public falling event, repeated several times since, told me that something was not right. I have never figured out why I had these falls, but I have developed a fear of going down stairs and I now always use a railing when using stairs. My fear of falling is metaphorical as well as physical.

In the journal entry that follows, written several years ago, I describe how precarious the journey toward self-understanding can feel.

# Fear Of Falling (Journal Entry)

Just in time for Halloween, I'd like to talk about my fears. For me, recovery is a precarious perch from which I experience the same fear of falling that I have had, in the tangible world, for several years. I was talking to a friend who said that fear of falling was the most life limiting problem of old people. It is the nature of fear to bring the boundaries of one's life closer and closer until one is suffocating in one's own security blanket.

I don't know whether to blame medications or my bifocals, but I have had some nasty falls over the past few years. I have fallen downstairs, over numerous curbs and for no apparent reason. I fell in a subway in Hong Kong, cracking my front tooth and making a spectacle of myself, the big blonde American woman bleeding on the floor of the subway car. Just this month, I have had two dramatic falls. The bruises and scabs from the first fall were still healing when I fell, sprawling, this time in a parking garage. I think I am getting an inkling of what an abused wife feels like, aches and pains and bruises a constant reminder of the last trauma, dreading the next one but fully expecting it.

Going down stairs without a railing is heart-stoppingly scary. I also have a deep, well-founded fear of falling into an extreme mood. I have this strange sensation of vertigo as I sit precariously on this perch called recovery. When visiting Colorado several years ago, I hiked with some friends to the Continental Divide. We had walked breathlessly through the thin air for what seemed like hours when suddenly an enormous canyon came into view. Even though the weather on the mountainside had been mild on that June day, the divide itself took our breath away, literally as well as figuratively. The winds, calm on the mountainside, were gale force at the edge of the canyon, nearly sweeping us into its depths the moment we peaked our heads over the edge. This awe-inspiring event was symbolically like my average day. Things are always a little precarious for me. The mountain beckons on one side and the abyss tries to sweep me in and swallow me up on the other. Yes, I fear falling more than almost anything.

Fear of falling is a metaphor for the constant, daily concerns associated with managing psychiatric symptoms of depression, paranoia, and mania. This fear results in ongoing monitoring of my activities, reactions, thoughts, and feelings. Fear of falling impacts my sense of self with constant worry about not only moods, but my entire sense of self. Do you have any metaphors for your fears? Your joys? How would you express a deep concern of yours in writing?

We've come full circle: I have resigned myself to the fact that recovery, for me, does not equal getting better. Recovery is, instead, the process of coming home to facts such as this one: I need to rely on others as a barometer of my behavior. Sure, I catch myself sooner than I once did, and I can soothe myself with the knowledge that these are—simply, but profoundly—symptoms, as real and as dire as heart palpitations or a spike in one's blood sugar. Knowing I am having a psychiatric "moment" does not stop the parade of symptoms any more than a diabetic could prevent a health crisis just by reminding themselves that this kind of thing happens to diabetics. There is no controlling the psychological waves that roll over me as the seasons change, the time zones change, as subtle things in the inner and outer environment change such as the weather, or the intricate workings of hormones, neurotransmitters, hydration, and nutrition. Or even serendipity. No. It means seeing the behavior, acknowledging it, embracing it, then laughing it off. Sometimes it also means having to say "I'm sorry." In other words, recovery doesn't mean that I am out of the woods. Recovery is recognizing the behaviors and thoughts as symptoms, especially when I can't control them. It is recognizing the worst of who I am and accepting myself anyway.

Wait a minute. Back up. Did you say recovery is recognizing symptoms as symptoms? Yes. For me, this is one of the hardest parts. Even now, when I feel paranoid, in my mind, it is still because of the hateful conspiracy "out there," not the one "in here." When I blow up and say a bunch of stupid stuff, it doesn't dawn on me that my lithium levels might be low. No, the person at the other end of the phone is a jerk. The problem is "out there," not "in here." It is the most uncanny sensation to take it on faith alone that these are symptoms. It's like looking at the color blue and trying to convince oneself that the color is actually red. It's difficult to imagine and impossible to see.

The mind is such a wonderful organ—my favorite organ, if one is permitted to have favorites. Yet it is not very good at monitoring itself, and it balks at calling blue, red. Figuring out what is going on in one's head is a Herculean task. Take understanding symptoms, for example. Andrew Solomon, author of the 2015 book titled *The Noonday Demon: The Atlas of Depression,* states a profound truth as relayed to him by a friend who deals with (and suffers from) psychiatric symptoms:

> Depression is a search for invalidation. And you can always find as much as you want. When you're depressed, you keep seeking to prove that you are unworthy.
>
> As self-assured, quick, and facile the manic mind is, its polar opposite, the depressed mind, is invalidating.

I have to agree. Your mind will always provide support for what it imagines is real. The brain doesn't as readily respond to the objective environment. Cues are re-interpreted through the distorted lens of symptoms.

## Differences Indeed!

If you are like me, gaining insight is difficult. People with psychiatric disabilities have the disadvantage of feeling things that others don't feel, seeing things that others don't see, and thinking things that others (presumably) don't think. If you are a person with a psychiatric disability, my efforts at greater insight into myself may or may not sound familiar. If you are a person who does not have psychiatric symptoms, you might find it hard to wrap your head around the convoluted processes in *my* head. Hopefully, it is clear that recovery is a life-long expedition and that symptoms come and go. They can be intractable, even when you follow all the good advice in this book. God knows, I have—and they are.

Understanding psychiatric disability as difference, gaining greater insight, and learning self-acceptance are the themes of this chapter. Thanks to good supports and strategies, I have been modestly successful with the first task, understanding my psychiatric disability as an attribute that makes me different (not worse, not better). The second task, gaining insight, is a task that has no end. I will always devote some of my energy each day toward self-exploration and recommend that you do likewise. The third task, learning self-acceptance, is a work in progress. My ability to maintain good self-esteem and a consistent sense of self is constantly interrupted by symptoms that seem to bounce around on their own accord. However, I have learned that even when obtaining a stable sense of self seems a remote possibility, it's still worth the effort to validate myself and my own experiences through insight-oriented activities like reading, writing, therapy, interacting (formally or informally), engaging in creative activities, and getting myself out in nature.

Life with a psychiatric disability means a lot of loose ends. I find myself questioning my reality, the intentions of others, and the meaning of events every day. I rarely come to any conclusions, even though I muster my CBT skills regularly to prevent myself from falling into a funk. However, I began this chapter by establishing a timeline of when psychiatric symptoms started and, throughout the book, explored what was going on during certain exacerbations or remissions. The timeline activity was very helpful to me because events in my life tend to just swim together when I don't pay proper attention to them. By creating a timeline, I was able to explore my childhood and the precursors to what later became a diagnosable disability. In various lessons, I have identified when I first had symptoms, what I was doing at the time, and where I was living and working. From there, I was able to map my life with all of the ups and downs of bipolar disorder. For example, I was able to remember who was around during each critical period of my life and how my symptoms affected them. I gave some deep thought to, and appreciation for, those who were allies to me when I was at my worst.

Insight comes with self-understanding, and that's true for everyone. Socrates is often credited with the following quote: "To know thyself is the beginning of wisdom." My hope is that you come to really know and love yourself, not in spite of your disability, but by embracing it as an integral aspect of yourself. Overall, through my journey, I have come to accept myself, quirks and all. However, it has not been a "one and done" proposition. I constantly have to work at self-acceptance. You may have to work at it as well.

My ability to write out my thoughts and make sense of them on paper (or on the computer screen) has been one of the most important strategies that I use in my recovery. At the beginning of the lesson, I suggested a wide range of strategies that can be useful in increasing insight. Here, I demonstrated how you can use one, writing, to figure out what is going on with you. Regardless of what approach you choose for self-exploration, I wish you deep insights, warm relationships, and a successful life.

Lesson Twelve: Insight and self-understanding are so important for recovery that I dedicated a whole chapter to the topic. The process of becoming a more self-confident, secure, successful person takes self-examination. I complete a timeline and examine my symptoms and fears. I provide many strategies and examples to help you gain greater insight into yourself.

# CONCLUSIONS: SO, WHAT? THE TAKE-AWAYS

*Working it Out* was written in a deeply personal and highly practical way, addressing both the tangible (i.e., employment) and the sublime (i.e., empowerment). I share the lessons I have learned from my experiences; sometimes painful, sometimes euphoric, often ordinary. Through work, love, friendships, study, and a career, I have developed an understanding of, and respect for, my illness and how it impacts my ability to work. I learn more about my strengths every day and have figured out what I need to be successful as well as what kinds of situations are going to trip me up. I share this wisdom with you with the hope that, from this book, you have new tools and insights to manage your psychiatric disability and meet your life goals.

After two careers helping people with disabilities find and keep jobs, first as a provider, second as an educator, I know a lot about the topic of employment and disability. I shared all of the strategies that have helped me succeed as well as some that I never needed to use, such as Social Security and state-federal vocational rehabilitation. Thank you for allowing me to use my own life and experiences to show you some new things, ideas that can help you be as successful as you want to be.

The primary title of this chapter is "so, what?" So, what? is a little joke I share with my students when I have finished a lesson and want them to work with me to synthesize the key ideas, to really sort out what they learned and why it matters.

So, what? sounds like a challenge, and it should be. The message in so, what? is that none of what we read and talk about is significant unless (a) the lessons were worth learning, and (b) the lessons have been learned. So, I'll ask you the same thing: So, what? What did we cover, why do the themes of this book matter, and what tangible learning can we take away from them?

In thinking about the so, whats? I looked for themes that were presented over multiple chapters and in a variety of ways. I used my skills as a qualitative researcher to distill some specific ideas out of many pages of related materials. Because you are not here with me to help me do it, and based only on my own understanding of these topics, I have condensed the lessons in this book into five specific take-aways: (1) Know yourself. (2) Know you can work, (3) Pay attention to support, (4) Add tools to your toolbox, and (5) Manage your symptoms. I explore all of these with you.

## Take-Away One: Know Yourself

The major task of recovery is to get to know yourself. That means identifying symptoms as well as situations that are problematic for you. It means having strategies at hand that you have thought through ahead of time and can use if and when they make the most sense. In every lesson of *Working it Out*, I talk about insight, both directly and indirectly. Insight is a big part of both symptom management (i.e., the intrapersonal, discussed in some depth in Lesson 12) and skillful means (i.e., the interpersonal, explored in Lesson 8). Developing insight is literally the backbone of your recovery. It is important for making decisions, negotiating relationships, and managing your life, in the biggest sense of the word.

You might wonder how to increase insight into your thoughts and behaviors. One of the tools I have used over the years is journaling. Although I don't do it consistently, my mind seems to know when it needs me to reflect more clearly on my thoughts and experiences, and journaling creates just this kind of attention. I have used journal entries throughout the book, providing example after example of how journaling "laser focuses" my thoughts. Another wonderful tool is therapy. You can't put a price on having a trained professional listen to you closely for an hour, reflecting on your life. The insights obtained with a good therapist can speed the process of recovery like nothing else. Consider it a gift to yourself. And, whereas therapy can super-charge your recovery, conversations with trusted friends and family members can provide a mirror that reflects yourself back to you. Sometimes you just need to get your values in order. That can come through Motivational Interviewing, journaling, therapy, or conversation, or can come in the form of a hike, a visit to the beach, or to a place of wonder (Lessons 9 and 12). For some reason, getting the big picture by immersing ourselves in nature can help put the emotional landscape in order.

## Take-Away Two: Know You Can Work

Knowing you can work means having a career goal that fits you well. A university career is a great match for me. Success in the university is predicated on what I actually accomplish, not just showing up for work. Productivity is expected, but no one is looking over my shoulder. If I work around the clock for a few days and then can't function for the next couple of days, the outcome is the same as if I had worked steadily on a project. Of course, I try not to do this as it's important to me to keep a regular schedule to control my symptoms, but I can't always help it. What have I learned from the unpredictable nature of my symptoms? I have learned to never procrastinate. I start projects weeks in advance and work on them steadily, always meeting self-imposed deadlines as well as external ones. In Lesson 7, I provided hints about how to assess career interests and skills, mostly by example. I provided specific strategies that are helpful on the job such as WRAP (Lesson 2), disclosure

(Lesson 3), reasonable accommodations (Lesson 6), medication management (Lesson 4), and help-seeking skills (Lesson 10). Work is a worthy goal that deserves serious attention. The process can be hard but the payoff is great.

The take-away? Spend some time exploring possible careers and accommodations by using O*NET, the Holland site, and the Job Accommodation Network (www.askjan.org). Get to understand your interests and your strengths and then take advantage of services like those offered by state vocational rehabilitation agencies to get retrained or find a great job. Not everyone is going to make work central to their lives and identities, but everyone should have more good days at work than bad days. Getting the right job is just a start. Like me, you may need to attend to those soft skills, skillful means, not only to keep the job but to move through the ranks (Lesson 8). I wrote at length about how to ask for accommodations (Lesson 6), how to manage symptoms (Lesson 12), and help-seeking skills (Lessons 10 and 11). These methods are tried and true--I have used almost everything I write about. Where I haven't directly used the strategy, I have researched it. I am confident that the skills and approaches discussed in this book work. I am sure that you can find and keep a great job and that a rewarding career is in your future.

## Take-Away Three: Pay Attention To Support

Support is multifaceted and includes both the formal and professional, and the informal and personal. This area, support, is often the weakest link for people with psychiatric disabilities. However, it is extremely important and is worth your time and attention (Lessons 10 and 11).

When I assess the supports in my life, my primary relationship takes center stage. My relationship with my partner has spanned four decades. She is that constant I rely on to steady me, to give me feedback, and to make me feel safe during the scariest times. I can tell that she has gotten weary of the mood swings and ever-changing symptoms. Sometimes I hear her sigh in resignation. Luckily, I'm often extremely productive on our various projects, I make pretty good money, and I'm a great cook. I think these attributes help her to want to be with me even when I'm making it very difficult for her to do so. Actually, we have a very strong bond that holds us together--I think it is called love.

Just as importantly, Sharon can be relied on to give me honest feedback. Recently she said "You're self-absorbed when you're manic and you're self-absorbed when you're depressed." We both laughed about this, but I took it in. Hearing from her about how my behavior comes across to others is enlightening as I'm usually confused about this without her input. Sharon has sometimes been able to redirect me away from delusional thoughts, but not always.

Besides Sharon, I am surrounded by friends and family who I can rely on, at least to some extent. Very early in the book, I coaxed you to surround yourself with people. These relationships are best when they are mutual--you help the other person, they help you. Cultivating relationships is a skill set onto itself. If you need more people in your life, a WRAP group or mental health group may fit the bill. Your professional support team is another crucial source of help, so consider carefully how you might utilize your psychiatrist, your therapist, or your case manager to help you build a circle of support.

I explore professional support (Lesson 10) and informal support (Lesson 11), encouraging you to surround yourself with professionals, family members, and friends that are going to help you stay well. So, the take-away is that none of us can succeed on our own. We need people in our lives to support us, give us feedback, and cheer us on. When these relationships are equal, it's even better. I know it's a challenge to find deep, sustaining relationships, but it's worth the effort you put into it. A good activity might be to create your own list of people who sustain you and what they mean to you. Cultivate these relationships and make them reciprocal. It's the give and take that will help to sustain your bond over time.

## Takeaway Four: Add Tools To Your Toolbox

In this book, I described and discussed a wide range of strategies, most of which I have found useful in my own life and career. My intention has been two-fold: to clearly describe the experience of mental illness so that your loved ones can better understand you, and to provide a wide range of strategies that will help you obtain and maintain a career of your choosing. The focus on employment is intentional, although most of the strategies can be used in personal, social, and recreational contexts as well. In the 12 preceding lessons, I specifically covered the following strategies:

- How to "recover" from mental illness (Lesson 1)
- Wellness Recovery Action Plan (WRAP) (Lesson 2)
- Disclosure of disability (Lesson 3)
- Medication management (Lesson 4)
- Weight control strategies (Lesson 5)
- Accommodations in the workplace (Lesson 6)
- Career development (Lesson 7, Lesson 8)
- Cognitive Behavioral Therapy (CBT) (Lesson 9)
- Motivational Interviewing (MI) (Lesson 9)
- Professional help (Lesson 9, Lesson 10)
- Shared Decision-making (Lesson 10)
- The critical importance of relationships and support (Lesson 11)
- Building insight (Lesson 12)

However, I feel this is just a beginning. Like it or not, having a psychiatric disability may mean that you need to try harder and work harder at things that are easy for others. Thanks to psychiatric rehabilitation, we have tools. As an individual, you may find some of these very useful and others not so much. You may need different tools, so seek them out and make them part of your life.

## Take-Away Five: Manage Your Symptoms

No one can manage your symptoms but you. A big part of managing symptoms is recognizing them for what they are. Of all my symptoms, paranoia is the most intractible. Why? Because I don't always recognize the feelings of alienation and suspicion as symptoms. Instead, I tend to externalize my experience, assuming that specific other people are bad or untrustworthy rather than realizing that my paranoid thoughts have created a false narrative. WRAP, discussed in Lesson 2, is the perfect approach to learn to recognize and manage symptoms. And symptom management is one situation in which it is imperative to have people you trust who can honestly and helpfully give you their perspective on your thoughts and behaviors. Be careful, though. I know people who would love nothing more than to have a say when it comes to my life, thoughts, and behaviors. Choose wisely. Not everyone "does" support the same way. Some supporters can be hands-off, assisting you in subtle ways. Other people are ready to take over your life if given the opportunity. Knowing your friends, family members, and supporters will help you determine who you would like in what role.

It takes a certain amount of practice and insight to recognize symptoms as symptoms and accurate perceptions as accurate perceptions. Ideas about how to gain deeper insight are explored in Lesson 12. I think a major task of recovery is learning to evaluate your own behaviors, moods, and thoughts in an honest and self-compassionate way. At first it will be very confusing to sort this information out, but it gets easier. With work on your WRAP, good therapy, appropriate medications, helpful feedback, and reflection, this task will be more manageable over time.

# In Closing

This book is based on the principles and processes of psychiatric rehabilitation. Psychiatric rehabilitation, a system of knowledge and practice that draws on both the best in mental health treatment and the successes of rehabilitation services. In many ways, psychiatric rehabilitation and recovery are intertwined: recovery comes about when you apply helpful strategies to your life. Psychiatric rehabilitation is comprised of the tried and true strategies that work. Psychiatric rehabilitation includes the following proven practices:

- Health and wellness services
- Intensive case management services
- Services for people with co-occurring disorders (both psychiatric and substance use disorder)
- Residential and independent living services
- Symptom management services such as WRAP
- Employment services
- Supported education
- Evidence-based counseling services such as CBT and MI
- Integration of services with family supports

I'm sure I have forgotten some of the many aspects of psychiatric rehabilitation as it addresses all of the parts of life that are affected if or when you become ill. This is the material I teach, research, and live. In this book, I have told my story in order to put a very human face on these abstract constructs and to show that even individuals with active symptoms can succeed in the world of work. It probably doesn't make sense to wait until you are symptom free—if I had done that, I would have been unemployed since 1984. Work is strong therapy in and of itself.

Helping people in recovery move from dependency to full employment is an incredible experience. I spent my first career as a job placement professional. It was exciting to figure out exactly what someone wanted and needed in a job and to develop a position that was a great fit for employer and employee alike. I feel similarly about sharing this book with you. I'm excited to impart knowledge and skills that I know will work.

We know so much about what helps people who want to work that these ideas should be part of every school curriculum, in every career center, and readily available to anyone who needs it. However, this is not the case. Psychiatric rehabilitation and recovery are addressed by relatively few professionals. Indeed, most counselors don't know anything about it. That is one of the reasons why I wrote this book: It is a guide to rehabilitation and recovery and it provides a starting point for getting your own life and career off the ground.

Having battled symptoms of bipolar disorder for my entire adult life, I know a bit about symptoms, symptom management, and "suiting up and showing up" at work, even when things are difficult. Because I have studied employment and disability while applying the principles to my own life, I am certain that these strategies are effective, and I have highlighted the ones that have worked for me. My hope is that you will find tools that work for you as well, and that you are able to succeed in any way that makes sense to you.

I'm glad you read my odd little book--part autobiography, part text book, and part self-help guide. In a way, I am pleased to be able to use my life experience as a teaching tool. I have worked harder on my recovery than any other achievement of my life, including earning a doctorate. The fact that I teach and research rehabilitation counseling and psychiatric rehabilitation *and* utilize the skills I teach probably makes me an excellent guide for others who have psychiatric disabilities and would like to work, or just engage in life more fully. Personally, and professionally, I am invested in the approaches I have introduced in *Working it Out*. I encourage you to try some of the lessons I have provided for you. Good luck!

# REFERENCES

Ackerman, G. W., & McReynolds, C. J. (2005). Strategies to promote successful employment of people with psychiatric disabilities. *Journal of Applied Rehabilitation Counseling, 36*(4), 35-40.

American Psychiatric Association (2013). *Diagnostic and Statistical Manual of Mental Disorders* (5ᵗʰ Ed.). Arlington, VA: American Psychiatric Association.

Arkowitz, H. & Burke, B. L. (2008). Motivational interviewing as an integrative framework for the treatment of depression. In H. Arkowitz, H. A. Westra, W. R. Miller, & S. Rollnick, eds. *Motivational Interviewing in the Treatment of Psychological Problems*. New York, NY: Guilford.

Arkowitz, H., & Miller, W. R. (2008). Learning, applying and extending motivational interviewing. In H. Arkowitz, H. A. Westra, W. R. Miller, & S. Rollnick, eds. *Motivational Interviewing in the Treatment of Psychological Problems*. New York, NY: Guilford.

Baggs, Amanda/Mel (2021, October). You Tube. https://www.youtube.com/watch?v=4c5_3wqZ3Lk&list=PL70BB95AC2A07D6B2&index=3&t=13s

Basco, M. R. (2006). *The bipolar workbook*. New York, NY: Guilford.

Bazelon Center for Mental Health Law (2014). http://bazelon.org/

Bolles, R. N. (2020). *What color is your parachute: Your guide to a lifetime of meaningful work and career success*. New York, NY: Ten Speed Press.

Brightwayzen (2021, October). www.brightwayzen.org

Burn, D. D. (1999). Ten days to self-esteem. New York, NY: Harper Collins.

Canacott, L., Moghaddam, N., & Tickle, A. (2019). Is the Wellness Recovery Action Plan (WRAP) efficacious for improving personal and clinical recovery outcomes? A systematic review and meta-analysis. *Psychiatric Rehabilitation Journal, 42*(4), 372-381.

Cook, J., Jonikas, J., Hamilton, M., Goldrick, V., Steigman, P., Grey, D., Burke, L., Carter, T., Razzano, L., & Copeland, M.E. (2013). The impact of Wellness Recovery Action Planning on service utilization and need in a randomized, controlled trial. *Psychiatric Rehabilitation Journal, 36*(4), 250-257.

Copeland, M. E. (2018). *Wellness Recovery Action Plan, Updated Edition*. Sudbury, MA: Human Potential Press.

Deegan, P. E. (1988). Recovery: The lived experience of rehabilitation. *Psychosocial Rehabilitation Journal, 9*(4), 11-19.

Deegan, P. E. (1996). Recovery as a journey of the heart. *Psychiatric Rehabilitation Journal, 19*(3), 91-97.

Deegan, P. E. (2007). The lived experience of using psychiatric medications in the recovery process and a shared decision-making program to support it. *Psychiatric Rehabilitation Journal, 31*(1), 62-69.

Deegan, P. E., & Drake, R. E. (2006). Shared decision-making and medication management in the recovery process. *Psychiatric Services 57*(11), 1636-1639.

Fukui, S., Starnino, V., Susana, M., Davidson, L., Cook, K., Rapp, C. A., & Gowdy, E. A. (2011). Effect of Wellness Recovery Action Plan (WRAP) participation on psychiatric symptoms, sense of hope, and recovery. *Psychiatric Rehabilitation Journal, 34*(3), 214-222. doi: 10.2975/34.3.2011.214.222

Jamison, K.R. (1996). *An unquiet mind*. New York, NY: Vintage Books.

Marrone, J. & Galowka, E. (1999). If work makes people with mental illness sick, what do unemployment, poverty, and social isolation cause? *Psychiatric Rehabilitation Journal, 23*(2), 187-193).

Matthews, C.K. (1994). To tell or not to tell: the management of privacy boundaries by the invisibly disabled. Paper presented at the annual meeting of the Western States Communication Association, San Jose, CA.

McHugo, G. J. (2012). A ten-year study of steady employment and non-vocational outcomes among people with serious mental illness and co-occurring substance use disorders. *Schizophrenia Research, 138*(2/3), 233-239.

Miller, W. R., & Rollnick, S. (2013). *Motivational interviewing: Helping people change, 3rd Ed.* New York, NY: Guilford.

National Association on Mental Illness (2021, October). https://www.nami.org

Olney, M. F. (2007). Caught in a social safety net: Perspectives of recipients of Social Security disability programs on employment. *Journal of Applied Rehabilitation Counseling, 38*(2), 5-13.

Olney, M.F. & Brockelman, K.S. (2003). Out of the disability closet: Strategic use of perception management by university students in the U.S. *Disability & Society, 18*(1), 35-50.

Olney, M. F., Compton, C., Tucker, M., Emery-Flores, D., & Zuniga, R. (2014). It takes a village: Influences on former SSI/DI beneficiaries who transition to employment. *Journal of Rehabilitation, 80*(4), 38-51.

Olney, M.F., & Emery-Flores, D.S. (2017). "I get my therapy from work": Wellness Recovery Action Plan strategies that support employment. *Rehabilitation Counseling Bulletin, 60*(3). 175-184.

Pratt, C. W., Gill, K. J., Barrett, N. M., Roberts, M. M. (2014). *Psychiatric rehabilitation, 3rd Ed.* Waltham, MA, Academic Press.

Prochaska, J. O. & DiClemente, C. C. (1982). The trans-theoretical model of change and motivational interviewing for the fringe client. *Psychotherapy: Theory, Research, & Practice 19*, 276-288.

Red Book: A Guide to Work Incentives (2021, October). www.ssa.gov/redbook/

Saks, E. (2007). *The center cannot hold.* New York, NY: Hyperion.

Solomon, A. (2015). *The noonday demon: The atlas of depression.* New York, NY: Vintage

Rehabilitation Services Administration (2021, October). www.ed.gov/about/states

Styron, W. (1990). *Darkness visible: A memoir of madness.* New York, NY: Vintage.

Wellness Recovery Action Plan (2021, October). www.wrapandrecoverybooks.com

Wright, J. H., Turkington, D., Kingdon, D. G., Basco, M. R. (2009). *Cognitive-behavior therapy for severe mental illness: An illustrated guide.* Arlington, VA: American Psychiatric Publishing, Inc.

Zuckoff, A. (2015). *Finding your way to change.* New York, NY: Guilford Press.

Made in the USA
Las Vegas, NV
27 August 2024

94499273R10095